So

You think

You're Chosen?

Also by Jacques More

Will there be Non-Christians in heaven?

Leadership is Male?

Revival – The Battleplan

So

You think

You're Chosen?

By
Jacques More

JAROM BOOKS

Cover design by
Laura Hope and Grange Graphics Ltd

Printed and bound by
CPI Mackays, Chatham ME5 8TD

To the memory of my old friend
John 'LeBout' of Dorking

John loved all and befriended many.
He spoke to as many people as he could in one day.
He probably was the most personally active Evangelist I ever met.
And he loved table tennis: his doorway to heaven.

CONTENTS

PREFACE

The issue of predestination has occupied many minds. In this book I am addressing a doctrine that has divided the Church for many centuries both literally and theoretically. The only foundation that a Christian can rely on for his beliefs is the bible. However its interpretation is the challenge. I make no apologies therefore for quoting it abundantly. But for some this will not be enough because there will be the need to have a look at the original language. The Bible was 1st written in 3 main languages: Hebrew for the Old Testament, Greek for the New Testament and Aramaic for a few portions of the Old Testament. The main language that has mostly been translated and affects the reading of passages on this topic is what is called New Testament Greek.

So you will find me challenging some translation. And to this end I present the following note:

Due to the simplicity of reading, where Greek words are mentioned in this book the words are anglicised. So *ésan* is for the Greek letters ησαν

You will note I have used an 'é' (an accented 'e') in place of the Greek letter *éta*. Greek has '2' types of

9

'e'; the other being *epsilon* = 'e'. Similarly Greek has '2' types of 'o', for *omega* therefore the accented 'ò' will be used; the other being *omicron* = 'o'.

A PERSONAL MESSAGE

——

Who this message is for

If you identify yourself with any of the following names or phrases, then this is for you:

Calvinist; Reformed theologian; Grace Baptist Member; Unconditional Predestination (to salvation) Believer; Grace Theology; Presbyterian (in some countries); And, any such like.

This book is about this belief. Here you will find that the belief was not in the Church for its first 400 years. Therefore many of the verses you have come to know will be explained differently. So I recommend you have your bible nearby when you read. More so, if you are able, I recommend a Greek-English Interlinear. This is because translators since this belief arose in the Church have tended to slant and even add words which give the meaning this 'belief' demanded: As Jesus said '**wisdom is justified by her children**' (Matthew 11:19): Which raises questions of intellectual honesty for translators of the bible, since the Reformation in particular.

But, perhaps more importantly I urge you to emulate the Bereans of Acts 17, who checked out if 'these things were so' (Acts 17:11). Their attitude enabled them to learn from what Paul was sharing and thus discard what they had believed up till then as incomplete, inaccurate or, altogether false. Remember, even the raising of Lazarus from the dead did not persuade some of the Pharisees, so for some of you nothing here will help you change your mind. Did not Jesus urge the Christians at Laodicea to anoint their eyes with eye salve so they could see? (Revelation 3:18). This is the way we are made: in the sense that it is a spiritual law, if you choose to believe something, God himself cannot dissuade you. I plead with you therefore to consider making a genuine prayer. Indeed if you are so convinced why not look at this prayer, see if you agree with it, and then begin by reading the very chapter which contains it. But remember unless you make such a prayer your own or, emulate the Berean attitude you may not be spoken to. The chapter I am referring to is Chapter 20 entitled *Making an Idol?* The prayer is at the end. You may find helpful to read this chapter as it was written without reference to predestination teaching, but only as a means of identifying an idol in a believer's heart by the fruits explained.

Then, some of you will feel hurt or find it hard to take on board that what you have believed for so long could be so wrong. Then the process of re-learning is up to you. You can begin by looking how this whole belief system was not in the Church for several centuries, or you can look at particular verses that have in the past convinced you, or you can just start at the beginning and plough your way through. It's up to you. But, if at any point you feel this is too much. This is too difficult for you. Then, go back to that prayer and commune with your Lord again. Remember He really meant it when He said:

> Casting all your care upon Him, for He cares for you.
> *1 Peter 5:7*

This verb 'to cast' is translated from the Greek word *ballò*, so consider your cares as a ball and throw them to the Lord knowing He will not only catch them, but deal with them.

Then, stop reading. Wait for things to settle. Be patient with yourself. Allow the Lord to re-teach you at the pace that is best for you. Return when you are able.

> I will instruct you and teach you in the way you should go; I will guide you with My eye.
> Do not be like the horse *or* like the mule, *which* have no understanding, which must be harnessed with bit and bridle, else they will not come near you.
> Many sorrows *shall be* to the wicked; but he who trusts in the LORD, mercy shall surround him.
> Be glad in the LORD and rejoice, you righteous; and shout for joy, all *you* upright in heart!
> *Psalm 32:8-11*

> For the LORD your God *is* God of gods and
> Lord of lords, the great God, mighty and
> awesome, who shows no partiality . . .
>
> *Deuteronomy 10:17*

ONE

CAN GOD BE TRUSTED?

——

Of course He can.

A thousand times, yes.

No. A million times, yes.

Again, no: More than that.

Why?

Because any number given implies that adding to that number would mean He is not to be trusted. Like a million times and one.

So, again, I ask: Can God Be trusted?

Yes.

Jesus said:

> . . . let your 'Yes' be 'Yes,' and your 'No,' 'No.' For
> whatever is more than these is from the evil one.
>
> *Matthew 5:37*

God can be trusted. Yes.

Jesus mentioned this in the context of not swearing. You should not make an oath in order to show you are telling the truth. It makes sense that if you swear, in order to be believed, then the inference is you do not need to tell the truth the rest of the time. This is why it is from the evil one, as Jesus said. This is why also, last time I was in court testifying as a witness, I affirmed and did not swear. Isn't it interesting that the very book folk swear on, teaches not to?

So adding to the simple truth perverts it. Well did Jesus say:

> . . . unless you are converted and become as little children, you will by no means enter the kingdom of heaven.
> *Matthew 18:3*

Little children have simple trust and faith and mean what they say. As believers this does not mean there is a need to be gullible, but teachable. It means also there is no need to add to what is taught for that will affect the whole. No matter how many good eggs you have, it only needs one bad one to be added to make a rotten omelette. What God says in His Word is true. There are times that scripture explains scripture, but there is danger in reading in the light of something already believed or assumed. This adds to the passage looked at, and invalidates what it says. Adding to the simple truth indeed perverts it.

So, what am I to make of?

> . . . God so loved the world that He gave His only begotten Son . . .
> *John 3:16*

... [God] desires all men to be saved ...

1 Timothy 2:4

The Lord is . . . not willing that any should perish but that all should come to repentance. *2 Peter 3:9*

'Do I have any pleasure at all that the wicked should die?' says the Lord GOD, '*and* not that he should turn from his ways and live?' — 'For I have no pleasure in the death of one who dies,' says the Lord GOD. 'Therefore turn and live!' *Ezekiel 18:23, 32*

What am I to make of all this?

Simple, I believe it.

God loves every human being equally. Jesus died for every one. He desires each and every one to be saved. He is not willing that any should perish. When someone dies in their sin, He has no pleasure in it. It is no wonder we read:

... God shows no partiality.

Acts 10:34 cf. Deuteronomy 10:17

... God is no respecter of persons. *Acts 10:34 KJV*

But you may ask, 'Why do I need to say all this?'

Because when simple statements like the above in the Bible have to be read via another teaching it is a perversion. It comes from the Enemy.

It is like Jehovah's Witnesses or other cult, where you can not read the bible plainly, but need to explain it with the help of some outside teaching.

But, 'Surely' you may say to me, 'How has the above been twisted?'

Answer: There is an estimated 70 million Christians who are under the sway of predestination thinking. This has many names. 'Reformed Thinking', 'Grace Theology', 'Sovereignty of God', 'Calvinism', Other...

Basically it is the belief system that some have been chosen out of the whole of humanity unto salvation.

All the above passages are thereby re-read as follows:

John 3:16
Since there are many different 'worlds' in the Bible it follows that this refers not to the world of humanity, but the world of believers.

1 Timothy 2:4
God desires all types of men to be saved.

2 Peter 3:9
God is not willing that any of His should perish.

Ezekiel 18:23, 32
This refers to Israel only.

These many sincere believers are taught that God loves the saved and those to be saved in a different way than the lost. They are picked from among the world of people: Chosen from eternity past. Reference is made to an 'analogy of faith' as a benchmark by which to re-read passages of the Bible.

The sovereignty of God is all that is seen, at the exclusion of the '**self-control**' of God and His willingness to yield (Galatians 5:22-23; James 3:17). This aspect of God is missed altogether.

Any hint of a belief in predestination is opposed to the truth that God loves everyone equally.

Any idea that God has picked someone to be saved will always imply others are not picked.

What is the fruit of this?

Answer: Division and a segregation of people groups: The classic example is apartheid which is founded upon such a belief.

There is no assurance from the scripture that you yourself have been picked: And thereby are loved like those who are.

Whereas if you read the truth that God loves every one then He loves you too.

If you know you are hungry for righteousness, you have the assurance that you will be filled (Matthew 5:6): And Why?

Because you also know He paid for you. This love and this payment are clear-cut in the Bible:

> . . . He Himself is the propitiation for our sins, and not for ours only but also for the whole world.
>
> *1 John 2:2*

Jesus is the substitute sacrifice not just for believers, but for everyone. That is explicit. What about His love?

> In this is love, not that we loved God, but that He
> loved us and sent His Son *to be* the propitiation for
> our sins.   *1 John 4:10*

God's motive in the act of sending Jesus is love and since it is for the whole world and not just believers it is explicit that God loves the whole world and not just believers. Since there is no other simple conclusion to be drawn from these 2 passages together.

If still in doubt as to the above, ask yourself this question:

If God loves every one equally and Jesus died for every one then, what words would you wish God to use to say so?

God can be trusted.

Now therefore, let the fear of the LORD be upon you; take care and do *it* for *there is* no iniquity with the LORD our God, no partiality . . .

2 Chronicles 19:7

TWO

WHAT DO *YOU* THINK OF REFORMED THINKING?

———

This is another introductory chapter to the subject and a foretaste of some of the detailed chapters to follow.

The Bible is a book unlike any other: it is inspired writing by God. Such is the belief of Christians and it is with this understanding that it is used as the source from which all doctrine and teaching is based. Now, if it is inspired throughout, then it follows that it does not contradict itself. It would be impossible for a clear statement somewhere to be clearly denied elsewhere. There is a teaching in the Church today, named as Reformed thinking: basically the idea that God has pre-determined who will be saved. This I have come to see appears to contradict with specific statements in scripture. I therefore wish to share with you what I have found in the Bible which helps me to believe other than Reformed Thinking.

> [God] desires all men to be saved and to come to
> the knowledge of the truth.   *1 Timothy 2:4*

The verb 'to desire' here is translated from the Greek
verb *thelò*.

> The Lord is . . . not willing that any should perish
> but that all should come to repentance.   *2 Peter 3:9*

The verb 'to will' here is translated from the Greek
verb *boulomai*.

My purpose (excuse the pun) here is to show
that both verbs which together portray God's wish,
desire, His purpose and actual intent are involved in
the above passages. I have read arguments that one
or the other of the Greek words mentioned does not
display God's actual purposed plans which when shown
together as here disproves such false thinking. Indeed,

> . . . 'As I live,' says the Lord GOD, 'I have no pleasure
> in the death of the wicked, but that the wicked turn
> from his way and live . . .   *Ezekiel 33:11*

I have often used this last passage with the above
two to show that the wicked are not that way because
God wants it in any way. These verses to me clearly
contradict any idea that God has chosen certain
individuals to salvation: picking out someone always
has the implicit and realistic undertaking that others
are *not* picked. This truth concerning this argument
cannot be avoided.

Making a selection always requires a remainder as not chosen. John Calvin, a recognised advocate of this idea was honest and logical and clearly stated that this was the case (Calvin's Institutes III xxi: 5). If others are not selected and if they are unable of themselves to turn to God, that is to say, without His help in the first place, then it is incongruous to suggest the above quotes are consistent with this 'Thinking'. Indeed this teaching which I cannot therefore help but see as non-biblical makes use of many passages as a form of backing, but when looked at closely they are found to be verses used out of context or, mistranslated.

Actually I have seen words added to translations or implications introduced in translation which cannot be read out of the original language: Greek in the case of the New Testament. For example, to attribute an understanding that man is unable without God to turn to Him, God having not made the individual with a capacity to do so, and particularly as a result of the fact that we are all born in a world with sin, Ephesians 2:1 is often quoted: man is '**dead in trespasses and sins**'.

If a man is dead, it would make sense that he is unable to choose for God without God first reaching out and enabling him to respond in the process. An essential aspect to this 'teaching' because it is said God's subsequent action in the individual's life is what enables them to respond to God. Added to this the idea that God's action cannot be resisted, it follows that it is only because of God's choice that anyone is saved. And therefore anyone not saved was never intended to be saved.

Let's take a closer look at Ephesians 2:1. A look at a Greek-English Interlinear shows that the common Greek word *en* translated 'in' is to be seen in the next verse but not in verse 1: it does not exist in Ephesians 2:1 in the Greek text. Instead the words '**the trespasses and the sins**' are written in the grammatical case known as the Dative. In this sentence this serves to show that the 'death' mentioned was occurring 'by' or 'with' the means of the trespasses and sins. This is termed *the Instrumental use of the Dative*: the means by which something occurs. The person is to be seen as 'dead' *due to and whilst in* 'trespasses and sins'. And this is the only sense where '**dead in . . . sin**' must be recognised from the Greek. It is not therefore useable as a proof text to show death as total inability, but death during and by means of a particular activity. Thus showing an ability as present to 'not be' in trespasses and sins and this passage would thus be a proof text (so-called) for a remaining ability to choose to repent: real free-will. A fact consistent with the 3rd of the first passages quoted above. It shows an ability to turn always subsists.

Another good example is the passage of Romans 8:28:

> And we know that all things work together for good to those who love God, to those who are the called according to *His* purpose. *Romans 8:28*

Here, at least the translator was honest in placing the added word in italics: *His*. This makes the passage read as if it is God's purpose. The word purpose itself being translated from a composite word *pro-thesis*: a display in front of, a showing ahead/before. The context however mentions the individual's heart being seen by the Spirit of God and that it is out of that display that a calling occurs. This is hardly a demonstration of God's purpose, but of the person's, the one being called as a result. It is a response by God to the unspoken prayer of the heart which He sees displayed before Him, which is what made Him work all things into good as a result. This being the actual context, God is seen to arrange – to predestine – out of this foreknowledge *during* the lifetime of the individual. Nothing in the text implies this knowledge was acquired or realised prior to the individual's life time: the opposite is expounded. It is to him who has that more shall be given, not to him who has not (Matthew 13:12). Other mistranslations involve seemingly unrelated passages like:

> For many are called, but few *are* chosen.
>
> *Matthew 22:14*

This leaves the reader with the idea that although there is a calling of many, few are particularly selected (in some way). The word 'chosen' here is translated from the Greek *eklektos*. A look at the way it is used in the Greek version of the Old Testament, the Bible of the first Christians (known as the Septuagint) is

25

interesting. It shows the predominant flavour for this word as emphasising *quality*: best, tops, etc. It is used of the fat cows coming out of the Nile in Joseph's dream (choice meat), of young men (i.e. in their prime), the pleasant land, choice silver, etc. Suffice to say that it is wholly reasonable and accurate to translate the passage in question *without any implication* of a selection being meant. It is correctly read as '**many are called few are quality** [fit/choice (i.e. worthy of that calling)]' (JM).

There are other passages used out of context like '**No one can come to Me unless the Father who sent Me draws him**' (John 6:44) or, '**you did not choose Me, but I chose you**' (John 15:16). Let alone other translation inaccuracies like '**such as should be saved**' (Acts 2:47 KJV; the same tense is translated correctly and differently elsewhere in the same Bible, showing a bias by the translator in this passage).

To demonstrate these claims of mine you will find separate chapters on each aspect or passage or even just the one word mentioned. For the word *eklektos* my previous publication in booklet format details every place the word is found in the Septuagint. It is provided here in full as appendix 2. I have also written a booklet *Romans 8:28 in Context* and the major contents are in this book as chapter 11.

There is a chapter on *Such as should be saved*. The following chapter expands on passages just mentioned as *Out of Context*. Then I will highlight in another entitled *The Early Church Fathers and Predestination* that for about 400 years the Early Church did not have 'unconditional election' as a teaching.

Later on I then ask *Who has resisted God's will?* Introducing by this Romans 9 which itself will be dealt with in a fuller chapter entitled *Understanding Romans 9*.

Finally I close near the end with *Journey into Light* demonstrating the life of God in every human.

This is just a foretaste of more to come.

> **For there is no partiality with God.**
>
> *Romans 2:11*

OUT OF CONTEXT

John 6:65, John 15:16, Acts 18:27, Acts 13:48

_____

The aim of this chapter is to explain the verses above within their context. This is to show that the way they are sometimes used (and sometimes translated) differs from the way they are understood in that context. I will first quote the verse as commonly found, then state how it is sometimes used following which I will highlight the Greek from which it is translated or the context, or both, to show how this differs from the original idea expressed upon the verse.

John 6:65

> . . . no one can come to Me unless it has been granted
> to him by My Father.

This verse is used to back the idea that God the Father chooses certain persons unlike others to come to know the Lord Jesus: They are said to be individually predestined by God for that purpose and others are said to be excluded from this encounter by God's own choice: Unless, it has been granted by the Father.

In the first portion of this verse Jesus says '**I have said to you that . . .**' alluding to a previous mention of the above. The previous mention is in verse 44 '**No one can come to Me unless the Father who sent Me draws him; and I will raise him up at the last day.**' Understandably this verse is used just as forcefully to 'prove' the idea mentioned.

The context that is left unspoken however involves verse 45 '**It is written in the prophets, "*And they shall all be taught by God.*" Therefore everyone who has heard and learned from the Father comes to Me**'. Here we find Jesus explaining what He has just stated above. God is in the business of teaching about spiritual truths and those who learn these things come to Jesus. Jesus did not say everyone who has heard from the Father come to Him, but everyone who has heard and learned come to Him. The implication exists therefore that you can hear, but reject and refuse to learn. This is Jesus' own explanation and there is no idea implied of a fixed number of people as being taught by God. Quite the opposite in fact, Jesus' quote says '***they shall all be taught by God***'; hardly a limited number. The context therefore of the verse in hand does not warrant use for the idea of individual predestination excluding others.

John 15:16

> You did not choose Me, but I chose you and appointed you . . .

This verse is used to say that God chooses every individual believer and they themselves do not choose to follow God.

It is of note that chapter divisions were not put into the Bible until the 13th century and verses not until the 16th. Here Jesus is speaking to His disciples. The scene is set for us in the beginning of John 13 where the 12 apostles are gathered with Jesus for the Passover meal. They have the meal (John 13:1, 2), Jesus then carries out the washing of the feet of each of them (13:4-11), Judas Iscariot leaves the room (13:30), and Jesus carries on speaking to the 11 until John 16:33 where He then prays to the Father (17:1-26) prior to going on with them to the garden of Gethsemane in the first verse of chapter 18. So, John 15:16 can be seen as spoken by Jesus specifically to the 11 apostles without Judas Iscariot being present.

If we refer to Luke 6:12-16 we can see that Jesus **'went out to the mountain to pray, and continued all night in prayer to God. And when it was day, He called His disciples *to Him*; and from them He chose twelve whom He also named apostles'**. Jesus specifically chose each of the twelve for tasks He had in mind for them. It is unwise therefore to refer this verse to all believers to prove a particular calling by

God which would exclude others (i.e. from salvation). They were appointed to '**bear fruit**': Hardly a reference to salvation (John 15:16 continuing).

Acts 18:27

> [Apollos] greatly helped those who had believed through grace . . .

This verse is used to defend the concept that faith is a gift of God since it is through grace that the folks, as mentioned believed, and this can only be the grace (i.e. the gift) of God.

The passage however is continued in verse 28 '**for he vigorously refuted the Jews publicly, showing from the Scriptures that Jesus is the Christ**'. The word '**for**' is an introduction to an explanation of what has gone before. Also the definite article '**the**' in front of 'grace' in verse 27 has not been translated but left out. So what we have (writing it the other way around) is that since, because, he vigorously refuted the Jews from the scriptures due to 'the grace' given him Apollos greatly helped those who believed. This is just like the way Paul used the word when he mentioned that he spoke '**through the grace given to me**' (Romans 12:3) and again in the same passage '**Having then gifts differing according to the grace that is given to us**' (12:6). So the emphasis on the grace is upon the gift and function of Apollos as a teacher and not the faith already held by the believers. It is through this grace (this teaching ability) given him that Apollos greatly helped those who believed.

Acts 13:48

> . . . as many as had been appointed to eternal life believed.

This is quickly visible as useful material to the pre-disposition that God chooses individuals to salvation and not others. The assumption is made that here God is implicated as the appointer to eternal life and due to this as many as were appointed by Him believed.

Just like the other verse in Acts discussed above there is a difference with the Greek text. The Greek here is as follows:

> kai - episteusan - hosoi - ésan - tetagmenoi - eis - zòén - aiònion

Literally this gives:

> and - (they) believed - as many as - (they) were - having (been) determined - into - life - everlasting

The Zondervan interlinear has this:

> . . . and believed as many as were *having been* disposed to life eternal.

Page 389 of The Zondervan Parallel New Testament in Greek and English © Literal English Translation Samuel Bagster and Sons LTD 1958.

'As many as were disposed' makes the appointment a self-appointment which makes sense since God, as the Subject grammatically, is not to be found in the text. Unlike Romans 13:1 where *tetagmenai* is also found but with the words added '**by God**'.

> . . . the authorities that exist are appointed by God.
>
> *Romans 13:1*

A self-determination is also in accord with the context because the verse in question starts with '**Now when the Gentiles heard this, they were glad and glorified the word of the Lord . . .**' the whole crowd of Gentiles, indeed '**the whole city**' (13:44) had turned out to hear Paul and Barnabas speak and the Jews jealous of this attention opposed them. This was such a confrontation that Paul and Barnabas then said '**It was necessary that the word of God should be spoken to you first; but since you reject it, and judge yourselves unworthy of everlasting life, behold, we turn to the Gentiles**' (13:46) and they quoted a scripture to show the validity of this. At hearing this, and this is where our verse comes in, the Gentiles rejoiced and they believed, (but, not all of them believed, it was only) as many as they were (having been) resolved, minded, determined into eternal life. That is to say that unlike the Jews that were opposing (and, that, was not all of them) showing themselves unfit for everlasting life, the Gentiles did not oppose, but rejoiced and believed (and that was not all of them): as many as were inclined to that eternal life already mentioned.

In conclusion therefore, in the Greek, the belief came before the explanation of how many, God is not mentioned nor necessarily implied as 'doing appointments' and this agrees with the context about the Gentiles involvement.

It is as if the format points to the writer (Luke), realising that he had written '**and they believed**' but already having mentioned '**the whole city**' was listening, he then adds '**as many as ...**' to limit in the reader's mind, any conception he could mean all the city got saved. This particular reasoning of Luke's intent was at first conjecture on my part, but it is no more as it can now be attested by his use of this method of explaining in Acts 5:36, 37 & Acts 10:45 i.e. '**as many as**' is added to qualify previous words alluding to *everyone*: Thus limiting the '**all**' which he first mentioned to a particular amount of people.

Writing material being so valuable, re-writing was not a worthwhile option, when a few added words now added (i.e. *hosoi* = as many as) removed the idea that '**all**' was meant as 'total' and this was Luke's proved practise:

> For some time ago Theudas rose up, claiming to be somebody. A number of men, about four hundred, joined him. He was slain, and all who obeyed him were scattered and came to nothing. *Acts 5:36*

35

This translation does not show the Greek which compares with Acts 13:48, so here it is:

> Hos – anérethé – kai – pantes – hosoi – epeithonto – autò – dieluthésan – kai – egenonto – eis – ouden

> Who – was put to death – and – all – as many as – were persuaded – by him – were dispersed – and – came – to – nothing

'And all, as many as were persuaded' Here Luke repeats the use of 'all' followed by 'as many as' to limit all's extent.

> After this man, Judas of Galilee rose up in the days of the census, and drew away many people after him. He also perished, and all who obeyed him were dispersed. *Acts 5:37*

This translation also does not show the Greek 'comparison', here it is in this case:

> Kakeinos – apòleto – kai – pantes – hosoi – epeithonto – autò – dieskorpisthésan

> And he – perished – and – all – as many as – were persuaded – by him – were scattered abroad

This is a repeat identical in practise to the previous verse with 'as many as' immediately following 'all'.

And those of the circumcision who believed were astonished, as many as came with Peter . . .

Acts 10:45

Here, the word all is not mentioned, nor is it in the Greek, but Luke's use of 'as many as' is clear. He mentions Jewish believers – that is believers in Jesus that were among the Jews. But, not all those who are believers, only those who came with Peter are clarified. This is the common use of *hosoi* 'as many as' by Luke.

Now when the Gentiles heard this, they were glad and glorified the word of the Lord . . .   *Acts 13:48*

But not all . . .

Kai - episteusan - hosoi - ésan - tetagmenoi - eis - zòén - aiònion

And - (they) believed - as many as - (they) were - having (been) determined - into - life - everlasting

The verb 'to be' in Greek is conjugated as follows in the imperfect tense (English Past Continuous):

ésen	I was
és or éstha	you were
én	he, she, it was
émen or émetha	we were
éte	you were
ésan	they were

Since in Acts 13:48 it is *ésan*, then it is 'they' (who) were decided.

In conclusion you may well have observed how important it is, indeed vital, to ensure when quoting a passage of scripture as a proof text that the context is in full accord with such an interpretation. Let alone the Greek.

Let's now look and see *IS FAITH A GIFT OR A CHOICE?*

FOUR

IS FAITH A GIFT OR A CHOICE?

Is faith a gift or is it a choice: what do the scriptures say?

Ephesians 2:8 is often quoted to say that faith is a gift of God:

> For by grace you have been saved through faith, and that not of yourselves; *it is* the gift of God, not of works lest anyone should boast.   *Ephesians 2:8-9*

If we remove the added words by the translator and look at a more literal rendering of this passage what do we find?

> té – gar - chariti – este - sesòsmenoi – dia – tés - pisteòs
>
> (Please note 'ch' as in 'chariti' is pronounced 'k' just as in 'Christ')
>
> The – for – (by means of) grace - ye are - saved - + Gen. = through – the - faith

39

For by reason of the grace salvation is yours through the believing

té chariti – 'the grace' is in the Dative. Here the Dative's purpose is to show the means by which 'ye are saved': the instrumental use of the dative = by reason of

kai – touto – ouk – ex - humòn - theou – to - dòron

and – this – not - out of/from - yourselves - of God/God's – the - gift

and this not of yourselves, of God the gift

touto – 'this' is in the Nominative thus refers not to faith (in the Genitive) or the grace (in the Dative), but to sesòsmenoi – the salvation

ouk – ex - ergòn – hina – mé – tis - kauchésétai

not - out of/from - works - that/in order that – not - [any]one - might boast

not of works in order that no one might boast

For by reason of the grace you are saved through the faith, and this not of yourselves, of God the gift, not of works in order that no one might boast.

Ephesians 2:8-9 JM

The question arises as to whether Paul is saying here that salvation is the gift, or faith, or both? This arises because he is saying '**and this not of yourselves** [but] **of God** [it is] **the gift**.' [Added words] The answer lies both in the grammar mentioned and in

40

his amplification of what he is saying in the following words: '**not out of works in order that no one might boast**'

Can one work for salvation? No, since it is by means of grace.

The thing is, Paul starts and concentrates on the fact that these believers have salvation, that it is by means of grace and that it is through having faith they have it; it is not earned by works, it is the gift of God. Salvation is a gift of God obtained by means of the grace of God and cannot be worked for: it is possessed only through [having] faith.

There is no grammatical clarity in the idea that the faith is the gift. This can be seen because if '**through the faith**' were removed from the sentence it would still make sense '**By the grace you are saved . . . it is not of yourselves but of God the gift, not from works in order that no one can boast.**'

If the salvation is removed what have we got?

'**For by the grace . . . through the faith not of yourselves but of God the gift, not from works in order that no one can boast.**' It makes no sense.

'**through the faith**' is a section of the sentence solely for the purpose of qualifying how the salvation is received. It is by faith. In fact salvation is a gift of God by that faith; as a result of that faith. It is not of works, lest anyone should boast. Faith not works precedes the gift. What gift?

Salvation

So to summarise: From the Greek it can be noticed that verses 8 and 9 fit together. What is not of works, so that no-one is in a position to boast, refers clearly to the salvation at the start of the sentence. We first see this in that *touto* – 'this' is in the Nominative Neutral, if faith was referred to then, since faith is in the Genitive *tautés* – 'this' (in Genetive Feminine) would be found (faith is a 'feminine' noun). 'This' is not in the Genitive.

It may be implied that this 'gift' also applies to the faith, but the word '**through**' from the Greek *dia* has the emphasis that it is '**by way of**' and helps to show that salvation is obtained '**by way of**' faith and qualifies how you obtain it: salvation is not something you work at, it is a gift of God lest anyone should boast. In other words, after saying salvation is obtained through faith Paul goes on to expand his thought by adding: indeed you can't get this salvation by working at it, it is a gift of God otherwise there would be something to boast about. It is no wonder then that we find Paul emphasising often in his writings faith in contrast to works as important to salvation. Which is why he often quoted Habakkuk 2:4 (in Romans 1:17, Galatians 3:11, Hebrews 10:38).

... the just shall live by his faith.   *Habakkuk 2:4*

Notice however that it clearly says '**his**' faith. Indeed Paul wrote,

> But to him who does not work but believes on Him
> who justifies the ungodly, his faith is accounted for
> righteousness.   *Romans 4:5*

Again we can read that it is the person's 'own' faith that is involved. But is this faith mentioned elsewhere perhaps as a gift?

Or, is it something which is decided upon: something believed by a desire to receive or hold such a belief?

Is it at its beginning, its inception, a work of God alone or are the individual's faculties allowed 'free' process to reject or accept any kind of offer to believe?

John says,

> . . . as many as received Him, to them He gave the
> right to become children of God . . .   *John 1:12*

This verse tells us that a 'reception' occurred prior to a 'release' of permission or authority to become children of God. If it were a gift than the right and authority would occur prior to the reception mentioned.

The Greek word used for 'received' is *lambanò* in its aorist tense *elabon* (past tense denoting occurrence without limitation as to duration) and it means 'to take', 'to grab hold of'. So this 'receipt' involves a taking hold of something for oneself and indicates a decision, an involvement of the person and this is prior to authority *exousia* – 'right' to becoming children of God occurring. The wording gives a clear cause and effect sequence. It is after you receive that you are given the right. This faith therefore is a choice.

1 Corinthians 12:3

Another 'proof passage' sometimes given is 1 Corinthians 12:3

> Therefore I make known to you that no one speaking by the Spirit of God calls Jesus accursed, and no one can say that Jesus is Lord except by the Holy Spirit.
> *1 Corinthians 12:3*

This is taken to mean that without the work of the Holy Spirit in a person, no faith is present to enable the participant to declare Jesus is Lord.

The passage in the Greek text shows clearly that it is only half of a passage and just as with Ephesians 2:8 above needing to be seen with 2:9 so here also 1 Corinthians 12:3 needs to be seen with the preceding verse 2. It must not be forgotten that verse divisions are a late invention and introduced in the 16th century. The first portion says: '**You know that you were Gentiles, carried away to these dumb idols, however you were led**' (1 Corinthians 12:2).

This first part mentions that when they were pagans, the Corinthian Christians used to get carried away, even as they were led (i.e. by spirits which were associated with these idols: 1 Corinthians 10:20, Deuteronomy 32:17). In the next section Paul contrasts this by explaining to them there are two clear tell-tale signs which show a person is speaking by the Holy Spirit: One is, Jesus will not be cursed, the Other is that 'Lord Jesus' cannot be exclaimed without the Holy Spirit: in other words another spirit would not do this.

So 1 Corinthians 12:3 is not a passage that mentions or implies that faith is a gift, because belief in Jesus as Lord is not in question here, but instead being able to exclaim that 'Jesus is Lord'. This is why James declared that the devils believe and tremble, which is not the same as inspiring others to say so (James 2:19). They certainly believed Jesus is Lord; they just are unable to express it since theirs is a rebellious nature.

What of Philippians 1:29

> For you have been granted [the privilege] for Christ's sake not only to believe – adhere to, rely on and trust – in Him but also to suffer in His behalf.
>
> *Philippians 1:29 AMP.V.*

This is not saying that the faith mentioned is a gift to all the readers of Paul's letter, anymore than is the act of suffering on Christ's behalf. Instead, they are both a privilege as also translated this way to avoid confusion in other Bibles (LB, GNB, J.B.Phillips etc). The opportunity is what is given not the thing itself.

Indeed how true it is that '**. . . the just shall live by his faith.**' (Habakkuk 2:4)

But, doesn't the scripture mention *Such as should be saved?*

> . . . your own Master also is in heaven,
> and there is no partiality with Him.
>
> *Ephesians 6:9*

FIVE

SUCH AS SHOULD BE SAVED?

———

In the Authorised Version of the Bible in English, sometimes referred to as the King James Version, the phrase '**such as should be saved**' is to be found in Acts 2.47:

> . . . the Lord added to the church daily *such as should be saved*.   *KJV Italics mine*

This gives an implication that there are some who 'should not be saved' and that it was only those designated (in some way) that the Lord added to the church. Is this a correct translation of the Greek text one may ask?

Do other versions translate this portion of scripture this way?

The Greek is as follows:

> Ho – de - Kurios – prosetithei - tous - sòzomenous - kath hémeran – té - ekklésia

47

The – but - Lord - added - the (ones) – [who] *were being saved* - daily - to the - church.

I have placed in italics throughout the relevant tense translation N.B. 'z' is pronounced 'dz'

As can be seen the portion at issue is 'sòzomenous' a form of the verb 'sòzò', 'I save'. Let us look at a range of other versions and see how they compare:

. . . the Lord added to the church daily those who *were being saved*.   NKJV

. . . the Lord added to their number daily those who *were being saved*.   NIV

. . . added to them day by day those that *were being saved*.   RV

. . . added to their number day by day those who *were being saved*.   RSV

. . . added to their group those who *were being saved*.   GNB

. . . added to their number those who *were finding salvation*.   J.B. Phillips

. . . and the Lord was adding those *being saved* every day to the assembly.

Young's Literal (Robert Young of the Concordance)

I have just quoted from at least 7 English versions of the Bible and I have more which say the same including 4 different Greek-English Interlinear versions.

There are other places where the verb 'to save' is found in the same tense and it is significant that here the Authorised Version does not add '**should**' (along with its implication):

1 Corinthians 1:18

Greek: 'tois de sòzomenois hémin dunamis theou estin'

Because this 'tense' is a Participle [a verbal adjective qualifying a noun but keeping some properties of a verb], it is visible that the ending is different fractionally from 'sòzomenous' in Acts 2:47. There the '-ous' agrees with 'tous' = 'the (ones)', but in the Corinthians passage '-ois' agrees with 'tois' = 'to/for the (ones)'. Please notice how in no way this affects the translation of the sense of action (the tense) of the verbal part but only as to which noun it relates to: it is the adjective section of the participle which has changed. This tense has been translated:

> . . . unto us which are saved it is the power of God.
>
> *KJV*

> . . . to us who are being saved it is the power of God.
>
> *NKJV*

> . . . to us who are being saved it is the power of God.
>
> *NIV*

2 Corinthians 2.15

Greek 'hoti christou euòdia esmen tò theò en tois sòzomenois'

> For we are unto God a sweet savour of Christ, in them that are saved . . .   *KJV*

> For we are to God the fragrance of Christ among those who are being saved . . .   *NKJV*

> For we are to God the aroma of Christ among those who are being saved . . .   *NIV*

The word 'should' is not a part of 'sòzò' and cannot be translated by it. For the sentence to include this emphasis another word 'dei' would need to be added. This has the meaning of 'ought', 'it is necessary', 'should', etc. But, as you can see it does not exist in the Greek text quoted above for Acts 2:47. And since I have employed the same Greek text as employed by the translators of the Authorised Version it seems that the special meaning rendered is less to do with grammar than something else. It is of note that the church thinking in England predominant at the time was strongly supportive of unconditional predestination as a teaching. Is it unfair to suggest positive bias towards the doctrine of unconditional predestination was in play? I think not.

It is sad that believers of unconditional pre-destination today make regular use of the phrase **'such as should be saved'** in the belief it is a correct translation. If any belief is supported it needs to be from solid scripture passages which are not in question and of course, any such passage would need to fully agree with its context for the interpretation placed upon it. And, as mentioned before, let alone agree with the Greek.

> But he who does wrong will be repaid for *the wrong*
> which he has done, and there is no partiality.
>
> *Colossians 3:25*

SIX

THE EARLY CHURCH FATHERS AND PREDESTINATION

—

If the teaching of unconditional predestination in regards to an individual's salvation is erroneous, then when did it begin in the Church?

I once wrote an article entitled *The Meaning of Elect* In it I made mention that "**There is no record of a teaching of 'predestination of individuals' in the early church until Augustine came along. So for at least 300 years any such notion was not taught.**" The context of this remark was that anyone 'specially picked' or 'chosen out from others' was not a concept familiar to the first century Christian. This helps to define the predestination discussed as unconditional predestination: a choosing by God in no way initially influenced by 'the chosen one', but in being prior to the existence of that person. This is what I mention as foreign prior to Augustine (354-430): Which is in fact more like 400 years of the Church without such a doctrine.

In response to this Article, I received a letter from a believer of unconditional predestination which stated: **'Until Augustine, nobody doubted the Calvinistic view he propounded, so it was not until it was questioned did he have to write it down in detail, just as all the great creeds have been written down in defence of the faith when various heretics have come along thinking they know better.'** I understand the strong feeling this Christian Brother has in defending what he believes. It is sad however since to me this seems more out of a desire to believe it than out of a reading of the evidence, and the aim here is to share some of the clear pointers that the early church did not have unconditional predestination as a creed.

I will be honest with you that I have not read all the early church fathers' writings but I am here relying upon compilers of the history of their thinking who have read them and quote liberally from them. I will just submit their conclusions:

> In harmony with the foregoing views as to human freedom and responsibility, *conditional predestination is the doctrine inculcated by the Greek Fathers.*
>
> *History of Christian Doctrine* page 165 by George Park Fisher DD LLD. T&T Clark. Permission has been granted for these quotes from the publisher T & T Clark Ltd Edinburgh (July 1994). *Italics mine*

Inculcated means it was the *teaching urged or impressed persistently* by the early Church Fathers. Conditional means in God's desire for you, if you work with Him it will happen; if you don't want Him, it cannot happen. Which, of course, is true due to His Self control (Galatians 5:23). Immediately preceding this statement, but after his various quotes from the Early Church Fathers, Dr. Fisher states:

> . . . the renewal of the soul is made to be the result of the factors, divine grace and the exertion of man's free-will. As a rule, the exertion of free-will, human efforts in a right direction, precede the divine aid, and render men worthy of it. It is a doctrine of synergism. God and man cooperate.   *(ibid. page 165)*

Indeed reading Henry Chadwick's *The Early Church* (page 38) the index points the first idea of un-conditional predestination as appearing from the Gnostic sect, not an orthodox body of believers:

> . . . the Gnostics [placed]. . . the natural order at so vast a distance in moral value from the supreme God. The influence of fatalistic ideas drawn from popular astrology and magic became fused with notions derived from Pauline language about predestination to produce a rigidly deterministic scheme. Redemption was from destiny, not from the consequences of responsible action, and was granted to a pre-determined elect in whom alone was the divine spark.

> Permission has been granted for these quotes from the publisher Penguin Books Ltd (August 1994).

In fact, when the teaching of Augustine on these things came into the hands of one of his contemporaries, Vincent of Lérins, he expressed it as:

> . . . a most disturbing innovation, quite out of line with 'orthodoxy' which Vincent defined as that body of belief which is held undeviatingly by the universal church. *Chadwick Page 233*

Another contemporary, Julian bishop of Eclanum, expressed that Augustine was causing trouble because he '**brought his Manichee ways of thinking into the church . . . and was denying St Paul's clear teaching that God wills all men to be saved**' (Chadwick page 232-3 & 1 Timothy 2:4). The Manichees were a cult Augustine originally belonged to which advocated that:

> . . . the nature of man can be corrupt to the point that his will is powerless to obey God's commands. *Chadwick page 228*

This continuing tenet of Augustine theology is an indispensable part of his unconditional predestination thinking, but it is in open defiance to prior teaching in the church concerning man's free-will. Roger T Forster and Paul V Marston in *God's Strategy in Human History* quote directly from the following Early Church Fathers:

JUSTIN MARTYR (c.100-165 A.D.)
IRENAEUS of Gaul (c.130-200)

ATHENAGORAS of Athens (2nd century)
THEOPHILUS of Antioch (2nd century)
TATIAN of Syria (flourished late 2nd century)
BARDAISAN of Syria (c.154-222)
CLEMENT of Alexandria (c.150-215)
TERTULLIAN of Carthage (c.155-225)
NOVATIAN of Rome (c.200-258)
ORIGEN (c.185-254)
METHODIUS of Olympus (c.260-martyred 311)
ARCHELAUS
ARNOBIUS of Sicca (c.253-327)
CYRIL of Jerusalem (c. 312-386)
GREGORY of Nyssa (c.335-395)
JEROME (c.347-420)
JOHN CHRYSOSTOM (347-407)

God's Strategy in Human History by Roger T Forster and Paul V Marston Published by Highland Books 1989, page 244: used by permission of the publisher (July 1994).

They conclude that as concerns 'free-will' three recurrent themes are found in the early fathers teachings:

1. **The rejection of free-will is the view of heretics.**
2. **Free-will is a gift given to man by God – for nothing can ultimately be independent of God.**
3. **Man possesses free-will because he is made in God's image, and God has free-will.**

It is implied throughout that this free-will is always able to act, even if sometimes to a limited degree, irrespective of individual sin inherited or carried out. They also state that '**the only ones to reject it were heretics like the Gnostics, Marcion, Valentinus, Manes (and the Manichees), etc.**' Two of these heretical cults we have seen above agree with Augustine. Finally I give place to Forster and Marston for the concluding words:

> [Augustine's] difference from the early church was not a simple one of faith versus works. The early Christian teachers were no less clear than Augustine that salvation was a free gift. His point of departure from them is that faith itself was an irresistible gift.
>
> We must decide for ourselves whether we believe that Augustine, or the Christians of the first centuries, had the true Pauline doctrine. *(ibid. Page 287)*

This evidence helps to show the early Church did not have unconditional predestination as a doctrine (for 400 years); it does not help to show how they read Paul's writings in the New Testament which have been used to say otherwise.

I refer the reader to my later chapters which go on to explain the meaning of the various affected passages. In particular Romans 8 & 9 and Ephesians 1 & 2 and, I offer the Predestination Challenge: a challenge to be given any Bible text which has been used to 'say' there is unconditional predestination and not to be able to demonstrate it means otherwise. This challenge originated online, but since many passages are now dealt with in their respective chapters in this book, I have opted to place or leave in Chapter 19 also entitled *The Predestination Challenge* all the remaining passages.

I now conclude this chapter with quotes from each of the early Church Fathers mentioned above:

QUOTES

Quotes taken from God's Strategy in Human History by Roger T Forster & V Paul Marston First British Edition 1989 published by Highland Copyright © 1973 R. T. Forster & V. P. Marston. Pages 245-257. Used by permission of Author (March 2008).

JUSTIN MARTYR c.100-165 A.D.
Dialogue CXLi

> God, wishing men and angels to follow His will, resolved to create them free to do righteousness. But if the word of God foretells that some angels and men shall certainly be punished, it did so because it foreknew that they would be unchangeably (wicked), but not because God created them so. So if they repent all who wish for it can obtain mercy from God.

IRENAEUS of Gaul c.130-200
Against Heresies XXXVII

This expression, 'How often would I have gathered thy children together, and thou wouldst not,' set forth the ancient law of human liberty, because God made man a free (agent) from the beginning, possessing his own soul to obey the behests of God voluntarily, and not by compulsion of God. For there is no coercion with God, but a good will (toward us) is present with Him continually. And therefore does He give good counsel to all. And in man as well as in angels, He has placed the power of choice (for angels are rational beings), so that those who had yielded obedience might justly possess what is good, given indeed by God, but preserved by themselves . . .

4)

If then it were not in our power to do or not to do these things, what reason had the apostle, and much more the Lord Himself, to give us counsel to do some things and to abstain from others? But because man is possessed of free-will from the beginning, and God is possessed of free-will in whose likeness man was created, advice is always given to him to keep fast the good, which thing is done by means of obedience to God.

ATHENAGORAS of Athens (2nd century)
Embassy for Christians XXIV

> Just as with men who have freedom of choice as to both virtue and vice (for you would not either honour the good or punish the bad; unless vice and virtue were in their own power, and some are diligent in the matters entrusted to them, and others faithless), so is it among the angels.

THEOPHILUS of Antioch (2nd century)
To Autolycus XXVII

> For God made man free, and with power over himself . . . now God vouchsafes to him as a gift through His own philanthropy and pity, when men obey Him. For as man, disobeying, drew death on himself; so, obeying the will of God, he who desires is able to procure for himself life everlasting.

TATIAN of Syria (flourished late 2nd century)
Address XI

> Why are you 'fated' to grasp at things often, and often to die? Die to the world, repudiating the madness that is in it. Live to God, and by apprehending Him lay aside your old nature. We were not created to die, but we die by our own fault. Our free-will has destroyed us; we who were free have become slaves;

we have been sold through sin. Nothing evil has been created by God; we ourselves have manifested wickedness; but we, who have manifested it, are able again to reject it.

BARDAISAN of Syria c.154-222
Fragments

'How is it that God did not so make us that we should not sin and incur condemnation?'

-if man had been made so, he would not have belonged to himself but would have been the instrument of him that moved him . . . And how, in that case, would a man differ from a harp, on which another plays; or from a ship, which another guides: where the praise and the blame reside in the hand of the performer or the steersman . . . they being only instruments made for the use of him in whom is the skill? But God, in His benignity, chose not so to make man; but by freedom He exalted him above many of His creatures.

CLEMENT of Alexandria c.150-215
Stromata Bk ii ch. 4

But we, who have heard by the Scriptures that self-determining choice and refusal have been given by the Lord to men, rest in the infallible criterion of faith, manifesting a willing spirit, since we have chosen life and believe God through His voice.

Stromata Bk iv ch. 12

But nothing is without the will of the Lord of the universe. It remains to say that such things happen without the prevention of God; for this alone saves both the providence and the goodness of God. We must not therefore think that He actively produces afflictions (far be it that we should think this!); but we must be persuaded that He does not prevent those that cause them, but overrules for good the crimes of His enemies.

Also worth noting: page 249 of Roger's book – used by permission of Author (March 2008):

. . . In *Stromata*, Bk ii ch 2, Clement argues strongly that "**faith is not established by demonstration.**" Faith involves a choice and "**choice is the beginning of action.**"

TERTULLIAN of Carthage c.155-225
Against Marcion Book II ch.5

I find, then, that man was by God constituted free, master of his own will and power; indicating the presence of God's image and likeness in him by nothing so well as by this constitution of his nature . . .

-you will find that when He sets before man good and evil, life and death, that the entire course of discipline is arranged in precepts by God's calling men from sin, and threatening and exhorting them; and by this on no other ground than that man is free, with a will either for obedience or resistance.

. . . Since, therefore, both the goodness and purpose of God are discovered in the gift to man of freedom in his will . . .

NOVATIAN of Rome c.200-258
On the Trinity ch. 1

He also placed man at the head of the world, and man, too, made in the image of God, to whom He imparted mind, and reason, and foresight, that he might imitate God; and although the first elements of his body were earthly, yet the substance was inspired by a heavenly and divine breathing. And when He had given him all things for his service, He willed that he alone should be free. And lest, again, an unbounded freedom should fall into peril, He laid down a command, in which man was taught that there was no evil in the fruit of the tree; but he was forewarned that evil would arise if perchance he should exercise his freewill in the contempt of the law that was given.

ORIGEN c.185-254
De Principiis Preface

Now it ought to be known that the holy apostles, in preaching the faith of Christ, delivered themselves with the utmost clearness on certain points which they believed to be necessary to everyone . . . This also is *clearly defined in the teaching of the church* that every rational soul is possessed of free-will and volition.

De principiis Bk 3 ch. 1

There are, indeed, innumerable passages in the Scriptures which establish with exceeding clearness the existence of freedom of will.

METHODIUS of Olympus c.260-martyred 311
The Banquet of the Ten Virgins xvi

Now those who decide that man is not possessed of free-will, and affirm that he is governed by the unavoidable necessities of fate . . . are guilty of impiety toward God Himself, making Him out to be the cause and author of human evils.

Concerning Free-will

I say that man was made with free-will, not as if there were already existing some evil, which he had the power of choosing if he wished . . . but that the power of obeying and disobeying God is the only cause.

ARCHELAUS
The Disputation with Manes

> For all creatures that God made, He made very good,
> and He gave to every individual the sense of free-will
> in accordance with which standard He also instituted
> the law of judgment. To sin is ours, and that we sin
> not is God's gift, as our will is constituted to choose
> either to sin or not to sin.

ARNOBIUS of Sicca c.253-327
Against the Heathen: 64

> I reply: does not He free all alike who invites all
> alike? Or does He thrust back or repel any one from
> the kindness of the Supreme who gives to all alike
> the power of coming to Him-? To all, He says, the
> fountain of life is open, and no one is hindered or
> kept back from drinking . . .

65

> Nay, my opponent says, if God is powerful, merciful,
> willing to save us, let Him change our dispositions,
> and compel us to trust in His promises. This then, is
> violence, not kindness nor the bounty of the Supreme
> God, but a childish and vain strife in seeking to get
> the mastery. For what is so unjust as to force men
> who are reluctant and unworthy, to reverse their
> inclinations; to impress forcibly on their minds what
> they are unwilling to receive, and shrink from . . .

CYRIL of Jerusalem c. 312-386
Lecture IV 18

Know also that thou hast a soul self governed, the noblest work of God, made after the image of its Creator, immortal because of God that gives it immortality, a living being rational, imperishable, because of Him that bestowed these gifts: having free power to do what it willeth.

20

There is not a class of souls sinning by nature and a class of souls practising righteousness by nature; but both act from choice, the substance of their souls being of one kind only and alike in all.

21

The soul is self-governed: and though the Devil can suggest, he has not the power to compel against the will. He pictures to thee the thought of fornication: if thou wilt, thou rejectest. For if thou wert a fornicator of necessity then for what cause did God prepare hell? If thou wert a doer of righteousness by nature and not by will, wherefore did God prepare crowns of ineffable glory? The sheep is gentle, but never was it crowned for its gentleness; since its gentle quality belongs to it not from choice but by nature.

GREGORY of Nyssa c.335-395
On Virginity (368) ch. XII

> Being the image and the likeness . . . of the Power
> which rules all things, man kept also in the matter of
> a free-will this likeness to Him whose will is over all.

JEROME c.347-420
Letters CXXXIII

> It is in vain that you misrepresent me and try to
> convince the ignorant that I condemn free-will. Let
> him who condemns it be himself condemned. We
> have been created endowed with free-will; still it is
> not this which distinguishes us from the brutes. For
> human free-will, as I said, depends upon the help of
> God and needs His aid moment by moment, a thing
> which you and yours do not choose to admit. Your
> position is that once a man has free-will he no
> longer needs the help of God. It is true that freedom
> of the will brings with it freedom of decision. Still
> man does not act immediately on his free-will but
> requires God's aid who Himself needs no aid.

Against the Pelagians Book III, 10

> But when we are concerned with grace and mercy,
> free-will is in part void; in part, I say, for so much
> depends upon it, that we wish and desire, and give
> assent to the course we choose. But it depends on

God whether we have the power in His strength and with His help to perform what we desire, and to bring to effect our toil and effort.

JOHN CHRYSOSTOM 347-407
On Hebrews, Homily 12

> All is in God's power, but so that our free-will is not lost . . . It depends therefore on us and on Him. We must first choose the good, and then He adds what belongs to Him. He does not precede our willing, that our free-will may not suffer. But when we have chosen, then He affords us much help . . . It is ours to choose beforehand and to will, but God's to perfect and bring to the end.

So for the early Church Fathers before Augustine, as Dr Fisher stated:

> . . . the renewal of the soul is made to be the result of the factors, divine grace and the exertion of man's free-will. As a rule, the exertion of free-will, human efforts in a right direction, precede the divine aid, and render men worthy of it. It is a doctrine of synergism. God and man cooperate. *(ibid. page 165)*

So that indeed,

In harmony with the foregoing views as to human freedom and responsibility, *conditional predestination is the doctrine inculcated by the Greek Fathers.*

History of Christian Doctrine page 165 by George Park Fisher DD LLD. T&T Clark. Permission has been granted for these quotes from the publisher T & T Clark Ltd Edinburgh (July 1994). *Italics mine*

Inculcated: *a teaching urged or impressed persistently*

> And if you call on the Father, who without partiality
> judges according to each one's work, conduct yourselves
> throughout the time of your sojourning *here* in fear.
>
> *1 Peter 1:17*

SEVEN

DOES FREEWILL EXIST?

The belief in free-will is widespread in Christendom
but a significant number of Christians hold to the
view that it is not so. They believe man's will is unable
to resist the will of God. Particularly in the affairs of
salvation the individual is said to be unable to choose
for God: any faith in God is a gift which cannot be
resisted. Man is unable without God's first enabling to
turn from sin. Is this belief in accord with the words of
scripture; does the Bible agree with such an assessment?

It is all very well for the early Church Fathers
to believe in free-will and that along with conditional
predestination there was no other teaching until
Augustine came, but does the Bible really teach it?

Lament over Jerusalem
In the event that such a belief in a lack of freewill were
tenable, then it would be impossible to find expressed
in scripture a desire of God, a particular purpose of

God, for the life of someone or a group, as something which could not be fulfilled. This desire of God would not be something which could thereby be resisted and unable to occur. Jesus however refutes this by his very words over the people of Jerusalem:

> O Jerusalem, Jerusalem, the one who kills the prophets and stones those who are sent to her! How often I wanted to gather your children together, as a hen gathers her chicks under *her* wings, but you were not willing! *Matthew 23:37*

Jesus is saying that he often wanted to gather people together, just as hen does to protect, to shelter, to keep warm its chicks, but the people were not willing. Jesus desired and purposed this but they refused to accept. By their unwillingness they were able to resist the will of God. If this were not so, then there would be no reason in Jesus' sense of mourning over this state of affairs. He desired this, was willing for it, but despite all efforts by sending prophets and others, they continually rejected such desires and purposes of God. They were able freely to choose and used this choice against God's purpose. Were this not so, they could not reject this desire of God and there would be no need for these words of Jesus.

Total inability
The concept that Man's will is not free to choose for the things of God by any extent (at inception) arises

from the idea of Total Depravity or, probably more descriptive: Total Inability. It can at a cursory observation be understood why such a belief is held because '**the natural man does not receive the things of the Spirit of God, for they are foolishness to him; nor can he know *them*, because they are spiritually discerned**' (1 Corinthians 2:14), as well as the explicit phrase that man is '**dead in trespasses and sins**' (Ephesians 2:1). If a man is dead, it would make sense that he is unable to choose for God without God first reaching out and enabling him to respond in the process. It would be like God breathing life into the dead in order to allow more life to be generated by a response (from then on). This makes the assumption, obviously not shared by Jesus in his words above, that this dead-ness is of a kind which prevents Man from turning from sin and thus towards God by some choice of his own; that is, without 'outside' intervention.

Dead in sin

What about the '**dead in trespasses and sins**' passage then? (Ephesians 2:1). I responded to the use of this passage this way in an earlier chapter. I think it is worth repeating. A look at a Greek-English interlinear shows that the common Greek word *en* translated 'in' is to be seen in the next verse but not in verse 1: it does not exist in Ephesians 2:1 in the Greek text. Instead the words '**the trespasses and the sins**' are written in the grammatical case known as the Dative.

In this sentence this serves to show that the 'death' mentioned was occurring 'by' or 'with' the trespasses and sins. This is termed the Instrumental use of the Dative: the means by which something occurs: So that they are 'dead' due to and whilst in 'trespasses and sins'. This is the only sense where 'in sin...' must be recognised.

It is not therefore useable as a proof text to show death as total inability, but death during and by means of a particular activity. This passage then shows ability to 'not be' in trespasses and sins and would thus be a proof text (so-called) for a remaining function to choose to repent: free-will.

The use of parables
The Lord goes further to show free-will when he shared his own reasoning for speaking in parables. The reason was that those who were not presently following God (truly in their hearts), were able to repent. These had the freedom and ability to choose for God, but at the same time were unable to discern the meaning of parables due to a different deadness envisaged by Jesus. This deadness – an inability to grasp without further inspiration – is because their heart did not allow such activity of the Spirit of God (the lack of 'spiritual discernment' Paul mentioned of '**the natural man**' in 1 Corinthians 2:14 quoted above). So they were dead in this area of their existence, but not in the area involving the ability to choose to repent and this is why he spoke in parables. Thus without the

understanding, they would not repent and be forgiven. The hypocrisy in their lives which comprised of a heart distant from God meant this did not allow free movement of the Spirit of God to enable them to see (to discern) what the parables meant.

Had Jesus spoken plainly and not in parables they would have understood the meanings conveyed without the need for inspiration. This would have put them in a position where they could see their need to repent and since they were fully able to do so, Jesus did not speak plainly to them. He spoke in parables so that those who were honest before God in their hearts, allowing the work of the Holy Spirit, were then the sole recipients of the blessing. Which is why he said '**For whoever has** [already]**, to him more will be given, and he will have abundance; but whoever does not have, even what he has will be taken away from him**' (Matthew 13:12). Jesus says that if they had been told plainly (those who '**does not have**'), they would have been able to repent. Whilst in sin this ability always subsists, but spiritual discernment is not. The scripture Jesus quoted to show the validity of this ability to repent is as follows:

> So that '. . . *hearing they may hear and not understand; lest they should turn, and their sins be forgiven them.*'   *Mark 4:12 quoting Isaiah 6:9*

If they were unable to choose to turn from sin then there would be no need to speak in parables. This biblical fact shows us that free-will, an ability to choose to turn to God is always present. No matter how much an individual is in sin there is an ability remaining to turn to God by choosing to call on Him. Such a call would release God's power to enable a turning from sin by the synergy of the two desires: the repentant sinner's will and God's power produce an ability to overcome. God's desire is always to enable a sinner to return thus to fully aid and abet repentance. This combines with a man's choice to become a synergy of power to overcome. This biblical principle was taught by the early church fathers up until Augustine came along (4th-5th century), when he introduced the concept that the will is unable to turn to God without His prior enabling and when enabling comes it cannot be refused...

Therefore the above is seen to perfectly complement and make full sense of the fact that God has no pleasure in the death of the wicked and that He desires all to be saved without exception; God would like to see all be a part of his family 'group', but He exercises self-control and will not impose His desire upon the person not desiring the things of God: this is the whole counsel of God. Ezekiel 33:11, 1 Timothy 2:4, 2 Peter 3:9, Galatians 5:22-23, James 3:17, Acts 20:27.

The story of the Prodigal son says it all for us in Luke 15. In the context of replying to accusations made upon him for spending time with sinners, Jesus gave this story and it clearly shows God's heart: for all to be with Him doing His will and receiving his blessing; but he is unable to draw near to those who will not draw near to him. As also shown by the fact that, even while sin like a cloud separates us from God, He is still saying '**Let us reason together, though your sins are as scarlet they shall be as white as snow**' (James 4:8, Isaiah 44:22, Isaiah 1:18-19). God freely recognises that the ability to reason and choose, of a sufficient degree, enabling full repentance is a God given ability always there. And since it is given by Him to all, it is not something to boast about, but brings praise to him in its free expression.

Rejoicing in heaven
In Luke 15 we read the following:

> . . . there will be more joy in heaven over one sinner who repents than over ninety-nine just persons who need no repentance.   *Luke 15:7*

Heaven rejoices over a sinner who repents. Indeed it is very plain that God has no pleasure in the death of the wicked:

> 'For I have no pleasure in the death of one who dies,' says the Lord GOD. 'Therefore turn and live!'   *Ezekiel 18:32*

• What other words would you like God to use to show that it is not up to Him, but man to repent?

77

- Why do you think there is such rejoicing over someone who repents?

It is only that this is what God wants, but the onus is on the person involved due to the inherent genuine freewill within.

No more.

But, I hear someone say, does not the bible also say,

> . . . His dominion *is* an everlasting dominion, and His kingdom *is* from generation to generation. All the inhabitants of the earth *are* reputed as nothing; He does according to His will in the army of heaven and *among* the inhabitants of the earth.
>
> No one can restrain His hand or say to Him,
>
> 'What have You done?' *Daniel 4:34-35*

In other words, is not God's will always done?

Let's take a look.

EIGHT

IS GOD'S WILL ALWAYS DONE?

————

Does what God desire constantly happen?
Can it be that His pleasure is sometimes not fulfilled?
Can God's purposes be thwarted?
Are there limitations to God's sovereignty?

Scripture tells us that God '**desires all men to be saved**'[1], he is '**not willing that any should perish**'[2] and yet it is mentioned in the Bible that many will perish and thereby these are not saved.[3] This has been reconciled by the belief that '**all**' or '**any**' in these first quotes refer only to those whom God has chosen to be saved, 'the elect'. But if this be so then how come God solemnly declares '**I have no pleasure in the death**' of the wicked[4] expressing that his pleasure is not fulfilled? We also know that Jesus said how many times he wanted to have the children of Jerusalem under his care but *they* would not.[5]

79

Can it really be that the Sovereign God desired something and it did not happen?

We read, prior to the first prophesying about King David, that God expresses concerning Saul the previous king, that He '**would have established**' his '**kingdom over Israel for ever**'.[6] This is an expression of an unfulfilled wish.

Can this really be?

Does not the scripture say '**Who has resisted His will?**'[7] and '**My word . . . shall accomplish what I please**'[8]?

Scripture is its own best interpreter and looking at the context of passages, this will of God and this purpose however, only refers to certain particular situations in specific circumstances. They do not refer to everything God desires and wishes to happen. Were this not so it would invalidate the truth that '**God is light and in Him is no darkness at all**'[9] and '**Every good gift and every perfect gift is from above, and comes down from the Father of lights, with whom there is no variation or shadow of turning**'[10]. It is made clear to us that God tempts no one to sin[11], so that from these texts we can see that God does not will anyone to sin: it is never His desire or purpose for this. The opposite is true, God hates '**a lying tongue, hands that shed innocent blood . . . one who sows discord among brethren**', etc[12].

But there are many who do these things: they are mentioned in scripture and many are observed as such to this day. So it is clear that God's will is not always done.

But, how can this be?
God who is a pure Spirit produces the fruit of the Spirit which includes self-control[13]. His unchanging wisdom reveals that he is '**willing to yield**'[14]. Indeed Jesus described his character as that of a shepherd leading his sheep[15]; he does not drive them. The Spirit we are told can be quenched[16].

So, within certain limits there is 'freedom' to do things where Man is allowed by a permitted period of time 'ticking away', to go against God's will. This eventually produces the possibility that non-automatons are those who are in relationship with God in eternity, when he stops the clock and says 'right, you who have chosen righteousness, come with me!'...

So what we see is God exercises self-control and He does not impose His will on the 'areas' of freedom given for Man to choose. *It never means he approves or desires men to sin, but that he allows them to. God's will, in the area of personal sin is not done.*

This is why even to Christians it is written '**draw near to God and He will draw near to you**'[17]. God is unable by His nature to draw near to someone refusing to do so. In the same way Jesus said that God is unable to forgive someone who refuses to forgive another[18] [in their hearts]: Which is why also again to Christians we hear Jesus saying look '**I stand at the door and knock. If anyone hears My voice and**

opens the door, [then] **I will come in to him and dine with him, and he with Me'**[19]. This is saying that God's will, can be resisted in certain contexts (even by Christians); in other situations it is not.

Where it is not prevented is where prophecy comes in because here it is seen that He brings about what he says will happen: '**I have purposed *it*; I will also do it**'[20]. And this is done by inspiring some, limiting movements of others (externally) etc... With Pharaoh for example, when Moses approached him to get the children of Israel out of Egypt he hardened his own heart 6 times and then when weakening in that resolve, God hardened (Heb. Strengthened) it on a further 6 occasions. So God made use of his hard heart, and without going against Pharaoh's will, He strengthened his purpose to His own ends[21]. Later, when Pharaoh wanted to overtake and destroy the people departing, God slowed him down by limiting/inhibiting his movements in order to protect Israel. This he did by placing a cloud between them[22]. Thus, God's purpose is done. Another example is God limiting evil by instilling confusion by causing communication between evil doers to be thwarted: the tower of Babel is the classic case[23].

What if a man persistently does his own thing however?

If during a lifetime constant rebellion occurs against God's ways, then this brings about a judgment upon an individual such that their life is shortened. God causes an early death for someone wicked to limit the evil fruit in the world; this is then the limit of the wickedness for that individual: '**The fear of the LORD prolongs days** [heb. addeth]**, but the years of the wicked will be shortened**', '**Do not be overly wicked, nor be foolish: Why should you die before your time?**', '**wicked men . . . cut down before their time**', '**Bloodthirsty and deceitful men shall not live out half their days.**'[24]

Conversely there is a blessing of a long life to someone who honours his parents, etc[25].

So, scripture reveals that The Holy God never desires sin and pleads with men to cease from sin[26]. He plans events which he knows cannot be thwarted because he moves the limits placed upon men's movements and inspires others to bring about the fulfilment of prophecy.

Salvation for an individual is shown in scripture as dependent on the individual[27]: God has provided[28]; man receives or rejects: as many as receives Him he [then] gives the right to become children of God[29]. This receiving and believing involves a birthing out of the Holy Spirit[30].

Basically Jesus is by His Spirit the light that gives light to every man who comes into the world[31] and this revelation can be received or rejected by every individual[32]. It is this choice then made which qualifies the individual to become a child of God or to remain apart from God.

Assurance of salvation is gained out of a conscious living relationship with the living God enacted by personal faith in the Lord Jesus Christ[33].

NOTES

1 1 Timothy 2:4
2 2 Peter 3:9
3 2 Corinthians 2:15
4 Ezekiel 18:32 and chapter
5 Matthew 23:37
6 1 Samuel 13:13
7 Romans 9:19
8 Isaiah 55:11
9 1 John 1:5
10 James 1:17
11 James 1:13-18
12 Proverbs 6:16-19
13 Galatians 5:22-23
14 James 3:17
15 John 10:1-16
16 1 Thessalonians 5:19
17 James 4:8
18 Matthew 6:14-15
19 Revelation 3:19-20 & context
20 Isaiah 46:11
21 Exodus 7:13-14, 7:22, 8:15, 8:19, 8:32, 9:7, (9:12), 9:35-10:1, 10:20, 10:27, 11:10, 14:8, 14:17 & cf. *Understanding Romans 9* – Chapter 10
22 Exodus 14:19-20
23 Genesis 11:1-9
24 Proverbs 10:27; Ecclesiastes 7:17; Job 22:15-16; Psalm 55:23
25 Ephesians 6:2-3; Proverbs 9:11
26 Acts 17:30
27 Romans 8:26-30 cf. *Romans 8:28 in Context* – Chapter 11
28 1 John 2:2
29 John 1:12
30 John 1:12-13
31 John 1:9
32 John 3:18-21
33 John 3:16, Acts 4:12, Romans 10:9-10 see also my book *Will there be Non-Christians in heaven?* with *The Meaning of Born Again.*

NINE

WHO HAS RESISTED GOD'S WILL?

———

In Romans 9:19 we find Paul writing this question:

WHO HAS RESISTED HIS WILL?

Having looked whether free-will exists and if God's will is always done, let's see what Paul is saying here.

The answer is simple when we consider the reality that God does not desire in any way or expressly purpose anyone to sin. Yet you and I do sin, so this is something which we do against God's will. It is not God's desire or express purpose that anyone should sin, so we resist His will in our lives every time we sin. God's purpose in our lives is not carried out when we sin.

The question Paul asks is simply linked to his preceding statements. This is in the midst of a discussion concerning the sovereignty of God in the nations; the context is involved with *what God purposes to happen in the nations.* We can see this, both from Paul's quote in verse 17 out of the book of Exodus, and later in verse 22 re-affirming this condition.

> For the Scripture says to Pharaoh, *'Even for this same purpose I have raised you up, that I might show My power in you, and that My name might be declared in all the earth.'*　　*Romans 9:17*

> . . . God, wanting to show *His* wrath and to make His power known . . .　　*Romans 9:22*

So in God's purpose, to make a name for himself by the display of his power in the nations, his will cannot be resisted. But, in the life of individuals where the wages of sin is death, it is never God's will that any sin, such that, activity of this kind is the resisting of God's will for that individual. For the scripture clearly teaches:

> Let no one say when he is tempted, 'I am tempted by God'; for God cannot be tempted by evil, nor does He Himself tempt anyone. But each one is tempted when he is drawn away by his own desires and enticed. Then, when desire has conceived, it gives birth to sin; and sin, when it is full-grown, brings forth death.
>
> 　　Do not be deceived, my beloved brethren. Every good gift and every perfect gift is from above, and comes down from the Father of lights, with whom there is no variation or shadow of turning.
>
> 　　　　　　　　　　　　　　*James 1:13-17*

So it is clear, God never desires anyone to sin nor causes anyone to do so. Our deliberate acts of sin are thereby a definite resistance to his will in our lives, since they are done against his will.

Paul discusses God's work in the nations and individuals at their heads in order to show that God's favour is not dependent on natural birth, but on God's work (it must be remembered that the book of Romans is written to what is primarily a Gentile church). Paul is breaking the mindset of the reader concerning the idea that what nation you are born in guarantees you a place in God's good books: i.e. Jews are God's people, Gentiles are not. So he talks about the nation of Israel as birthed not out of the flesh but out of promise, and anyone who lives by faith irrespective of his natural birth background, ends up as a child of promise also. God in the full context of Paul's quotes has mercy on the merciful, those who live by faith, and he hardens the hardhearted. So that when Paul says, God:

> . . . has mercy on whom He wills, and whom He wills He hardens.   *Romans 9:18*

The context, referring to Pharaoh, reveals that for his purposes on earth God hardened Pharaoh's heart (Hebrew *chazaq* 'to strengthen', 'help', 'fortify'), after Pharaoh himself had hardened it. After Pharaoh had hardened his heart 6 times the Lord then stepped in and strengthened it a further 6 times to accomplish his purposes (I show this in detail in the next chapter). This strengthened Pharaoh to do what was in his intent to do, God used this to make his name known.

The mercy of God is also dependent upon the previous state of heart of the recipient when observed fully in context. Moses had been told by God as quoted by Paul:

> *I will have mercy on whomever I will have mercy, and I will have compassion on whomever I will have compassion.* Romans 9:15

Moses had previously cried out to God for Him to have mercy on the wicked Israelites (Exodus 32:30-32). God however had mercy temporarily on the nation and spared them for 40 years during which time the wicked unbelievers were weeded out. This is because God honours those who honour him and others are not (1 Samuel 2:30): Which is why Jesus said '**Blessed *are* the merciful, for they shall obtain mercy**' (Matthew 5:7). This is what the Old Testament also makes clear:

> With the merciful You [God] will show Yourself merciful; with a blameless man You will show Yourself blameless; with the pure You will show Yourself pure . . . *2 Samuel 22:26-27*

So all those who show faith by being merciful: as a natural fruit of their inward faith, will equally be shown mercy by the living God, and be recognised as sons of promise. And Moses' request that the Lord be merciful with all the nation, was replied to by God's express statement, that only those He deemed worthy would He have mercy on, and this was only whom He could see (as worthy of it). God's immediate reply to Moses was that only those who sinned against Him would have their names removed from God's book (Exodus 32:32-33), thus sparing Moses who was offering himself up if God would not spare the nation. But, by saying this God was also saying, not all whom Moses might have felt should be spared, would be. This is the immediate context of God then saying to Moses '*I will have mercy on whomever I will have mercy . . .*' (Exodus 33:19 as quoted in Romans 9:15 Paul was quoting the Septuagint – the Greek Version of the O.T.).

So as testified well elsewhere in scripture, the merciful obtain mercy. The wicked are hardened whenever God's name '**to make His power known**' (Romans 9:22) is involved. Such that the words of Jesus can be understood:

> For whoever has, to him more will be given, and he will have abundance; but whoever does not have, even what he has will be taken away from him.
>
> *Matthew 13:12*

As Romans Nine continues Paul then talks about vessels of clay which, God as the potter, is able to make into what he wishes. He only does this however, as a result and consequence of the inclination visible of the recipient. He makes harder those inclined to be, and as we saw only for a certain purpose, and he makes the merciful to receive mercy. The fairness of this can be seen in that God shines his light on every soul (John 1:4, 9) and it is those who receive this light who are then made into vessels of mercy (John 1:12). Those who reject the light pave the way for a hardening of their heart and associated consequences (John 3:19-20).

This chapter is a foretaste and thus an introduction to the issues brought up in Romans 9. Let's take a detailed look now.

TEN

UNDERSTANDING ROMANS 9

———

Romans 9 is a set of definite text out of context proof passages used to declare God's sovereignty in deciding who receives his mercy or not: because this is uttered as part of a package of belief that God has in eternity past chosen who is saved and who is not, this chapter of Romans is considered within that belief as hard core evidence.

The previous chapter should help for most folk not acquainted with it. But the thing is, this passage has been such a force for those who have believed in unconditional predestination as regards salvation, that it fully deserves a chapter of its own. So my aim is to concentrate as much as possible on the 'sticking points' in Romans 9.

I aim to show that in its full biblical context there is a different way of understanding the contents of Romans 9. This would then enable an appreciation of what was probably understood in the reading of this passage by the early Church prior to Augustine: for 400 years the emphasis of Christian writers was on a doctrine of 'conditional predestination' – see my earlier Chapter 6 on *The Early Church Fathers and Predestination*.

This chapter therefore fills a gap in the provision of understanding of this text. I recommend the reader therefore to read the portion of chapter 9 relevant before each section. Please read Romans 9:1-13

Romans 9

There is in this passage reference to salvation of a nation, salvation for individuals, and for a large part the use of particular individuals to bring about God's purposes in the nations. It is the discerning of which part of the passage refers to these different things which is the challenge to understanding Romans 9.

The section of Verses which are said to show support for unconditional predestination (Verses 7-23) are in fact not directly related to the topic of salvation of individuals, but instead to Paul's expansion upon the theme of '**children of the promise**' (Verse 8). This can be seen by the individuals he uses to illustrate the children of promise concept. He mentions the Jewish Patriarchs Isaac and Jacob and compares them to their brothers – who were not 'promised' – Ishmael and Esau respectively. Does this tell us that Ishmael and Esau are possibly not saved?

No. The passage does not allude to this at all.

It shows that God picked Isaac and Jacob to set up Israel as a particular nation, set apart from the other nations, not that the individuals themselves are picked for salvation and the others are not. God is being shown here as someone who decides what to use an individual's life for, in His purposes in the nations.

It is then that Paul the author of Romans talks of Pharaoh, who was also made use of by God to show His power in the nations. But, before I write of Pharaoh further, allow me to amplify some more about the comparison with the patriarchs and their brothers.

The Patriarchs

Before Jacob and Esau were born to Rebecca, Isaac's wife, she was told that the older would serve the younger (Romans 9:12; Genesis 25:23) and elsewhere we read that God says '**Jacob I have loved, but Esau I have hated**' (Romans 9:13; Malachi 1:2-3). But, is this referring to the individuals' lives or, to the nations that arose from them?

Well, did Esau serve Jacob in his lifetime?

And, does the context of the passage where God is mentioned as 'loving the one and hating the other' to do with the nations, or the individuals?

Is it to do with the individuals?

No. Esau did not serve Jacob.

But Edom the nation which arose from Esau did serve the nation of Israel the nation which arose from Jacob. And these nations are the ones being discussed in Malachi where love of the one and hate of the other is found. A look at Malachi 1:1-5 reveals the nation and territory of Edom and Israel, the inheritance of their founding fathers, is addressed. For example:

> But Esau I have hated, and laid waste his mountains and his heritage for the jackals of the wilderness.
>
> *Malachi 1:3*

It is also interesting to note that Paul's quotes from the Old Testament are taken from the Septuagint, the Greek Version of the O.T. (also quoted by Jesus), and using that same Greek word for '**hate**' *miseò*, Jesus calls on his followers to hate their father and mother, wife, children, brothers and sisters, and their own lives as a comparison to the love for God and the Kingdom which they are to have (Luke 14:26). But the bible also makes clear that a man must love his wife (Ephesians 5:25) and honour his parents (Ephesians 6:1). So it is only in comparison to His love for the nation of Israel God is seen to 'hate' the nation of Edom. The nations can clearly be seen in God's mind when He said to Rebecca:

> Two nations *are* in your womb, two peoples shall be separated from your body; *one* people shall be stronger than the other, and the older shall serve the younger.
>
> *Genesis 25:23*

94

So it is evident the Romans 9 passage here is not talking about God's election to salvation of Isaac, Ishmael, Jacob and Esau. Ishmael and Esau's salvation are not in question here. It is not talking about a choice of God to salvation of individuals, but of God's election to a purpose for certain individuals' lives in bringing about God's chosen purpose in the nations.

Please read Romans 9:14-16

Is God unfair?

Paul then asks is God unfair in doing this? (Verse 14 – is there unrighteousness with him?) That is, His acting in this way to pick out an individual above another to bring about His purposes in the nations: Is that unfair?

He says no.

And then says why. In explaining about those who are 'children of promise' and those who are not, Paul then begins a link to the idea of someone being a child of promise as someone who receives God's mercy.

By this Paul is thereby demonstrating that God is not unfair. He has not yet finished: to make his point – about God being God – in using people's lives for His purposes in the nations by His own election to do so. But, he does begin to mention mercy referring to individuals as distinct from a whole nation. This is mercy which as individuals are concerned does relate to salvation, but only by implication so far in the text, as further explained.

God's Modus Operandi

Paul explains God's fairness ('His righteousness' Romans 9:14) by allusion to God's Modus Operandi – His method of working – to determine who is picked for His purposes in the nations. There are 3 separate pointers in this passage to God's method of picking people for a purpose:

1. The first, who God shows mercy to.
2. The second, who God hardens.
3. The third, Paul's expansion on the mention of the potter and the clay.

1. WHO GOD SHOWS MERCY TO

With the first, God has mercy on whom He wills – it is not of him who wills, nor of him who runs, but of God (Romans 9:15-16).

Out of context this is easily seen as alluding to the idea that God's 'grace' is at work here (in the Calvinist mindset/belief the word 'grace' refers to God's picking 'graciously' some over others – again assuming salvation of individuals alone is being discussed by 'that method of reading'). In context however, Paul speaks of the nation of Israel at the beginning of Romans 9 as a people who he desired to see saved to the extent that he would be willing to be accursed himself if it could guarantee their salvation.

Paul is therefore talking about salvation here, but that of a whole nation, not individuals – it is the salvation of Israel as a people – this is where the different emphasis need highlighting so as not to confuse: where the salvation emphasis applies – and this can only be done with reference to the context Paul alludes to from the Old Testament as mentioned by him.

Paul quotes Moses' writing of God's words '*I will have mercy on whomever I will have mercy, and I will have compassion on whomever I will have compassion*' (Romans 9:15; Exodus 33:19). Paul then writes '**So then** *it is* **not of him who wills, nor of him who runs, but of God who shows mercy**' (Verse 16).

Now, if you read this on its own it can easily be seen as useful to a belief in a capricious God. If God has mercy on whom he wills and thereby no one else, it is language of decision about someone without that person's own actions having an influence on that decision.

But, Paul is quoting this immediately after stating and in answer to the question:

Is *there* unrighteousness with God?   *Romans 9:14*

To which he introduces the quote of '**I will have mercy on whomever I will**' with,

Certainly not!
For He says to Moses . . .   *Romans 9:14-15*

And then Paul quotes the words uttered to Moses. Surely, if this is a response to the idea of God being capricious and seeming unjust, then this quote of what God says to Moses is not going to reinforce that feeling but completely rebuke it. But it can only refute it in context: the setting in which God said it originally being appreciated. Without that setting it is not understood and has been erroneously used to say the opposite.

When God said these words to Moses, Moses had already pleaded with God to take his own life and spare Israel (the nation – Exodus 32:32): Just as Paul was considering in the beginning of Romans 9. Paul remember, explained his own desire also to be accursed, if it could mean Israel as a nation was to be spared – his kinsmen the Jews (Romans 9:1-3).

God however, is determined to be just and true and be seen to be without partiality and thereby, to the merciful (circumcised in heart), He will be merciful; to the devious, He will be otherwise (Psalm 18:25-26). God honours those who honour him and others are not (1 Samuel 2:30): Which is why Jesus said '**Blessed *are* the merciful for they shall obtain mercy'** (Matthew 5:7). This is what scripture teaches and Paul is not disagreeing with this.

> With the merciful You will show Yourself merciful; with a blameless man You will show Yourself blameless; with the pure You will show Yourself pure . . .   *2 Samuel 22:26-27*

So it can be seen in biblical context God shows mercy to those whose lives honour Him. He will in no way have Moses life be taken, but only those of the wicked. I add the next verse now and then go on expanding further that point.

Not of him who wills

> . . . So then *it is* not of him who wills, nor of him who runs, but of God who shows mercy.
>
> *Romans 9:16*

It is not according to 'who wills', that is to say Moses' will or Paul's will – since they *both* desired the same thing – mercy on the whole of Israel.

Nor of him who runs

Nor is it according to '**him who runs**', that is to say those born into the nation of Israel and dependent upon that fact, nor any amount of works of the law.

But of God who shows mercy

But it is '**of God who shows mercy**', that is to say only individuals (not a whole nation) who themselves show mercy as per God's Modus Operandi. They are the ones who receive mercy.

The expansion

God responds to the faith in the heart that shows it. For in that same 'breath' – that very quote about having mercy on whom He wills – God clearly said to Moses who He would not be merciful to: certain individuals whom Moses had included in his prayer for mercy for the whole nation: '**Whoever has sinned against Me, I will blot him out of My book**' (Exodus 32:33). The clear implication then is, 'But not you Moses!' Therefore we have a clear truth revealed: that those who have not sinned against Him – in context of a particular sin: 'unbelief' – *they* are those whose names are not blotted out of the book of life: to whom God is merciful.

But, is mercy here only to do with individuals within the midst of the nation of Israel?

No, because the whole nation itself was spared as expounded in Exodus. The whole nation was spared from destruction, but they were prevented to enter their promised land for 40 years (Numbers 14:26-33). They had space to repent – and if they did not, God used that time to weed out all those uncircumcised in heart. God spared Israel for a time, but the undeserving (the unbelieving) did perish eventually; the merciful did not perish (the believing) For example: Caleb and Joshua of that age group. So God's mercy was seen on the whole nation even if undeserved and this showed God's power in the nations. Similarly His power was seen in Pharaoh.

Please read Romans 9:17-19

2. PHARAOH

God is being shown by Paul as sovereign by deciding what He wants to do. Mercy on the whole nation of Israel for a time thus His name is not dishonoured in the nations. Moses had argued if God destroyed them the other nations would say that God took them out of Egypt in order to wipe them out (Exodus 32:11-12). But beyond that time only the believing are seen to have enduring mercy and favour. Pharaoh on his part is seen as someone whom God hardens in order to bring about His purpose in the nations and again, to make a name for Himself. Here then is Paul's second illustration to God's way of working.

> For the Scripture says to Pharaoh, *'Even for this same purpose I have raised you up, that I might show My power in you, and that My name might be declared in all the earth.'* Romans 9:17

God Himself as just quoted, clearly defines the extent of the purpose to Pharaoh being hardened (Exodus 9:17-18). It is solely that He might show His power and that His name might be declared in all the earth. This categorically denies therefore any assumption or idea that this very real sovereign work of God has anything to do with salvation leading to eternal life; it is only for a period of activity desired by God on earth. As far as Pharaoh being hardened, was this something against his will? Something which Pharaoh did not want to happen himself?

Again, going back to the sequence of events recorded we find that any hardening (strengthening) on God's part of Pharaoh's resolve to refuse Moses requests did not occur until after Pharaoh himself had hardened his own heart six times. It was not until the seventh occasion onwards that God enabled him, (strengthened) his heart to remain steadfast in its own hardness.

In detail, we have:

(1) Exodus 7:13, 14 (please note here that NKJV & NIV et al. are correct here and not AV – the Hebrew here does not infer God hardened it here – and not only that, but He had no need to do this early in the sequence of events) following the casting down of Moses rod and the serpent sign, '**Pharaoh's heart grew hard**'.

(2) Exodus 7:22 following the turning of the Nile to blood, the magicians of Egypt did so also and '**Pharaoh's heart grew hard**'

(3) Exodus 8:15 after the plague of frogs had been lifted '**Pharaoh saw that there was relief, he hardened his heart and did not heed them**'

(4) Exodus 8:19 after the plague of lice, even though the magicians could not do likewise '**Pharaoh's heart grew hard**'

(5) Exodus 8:32 after the plague of flies, despite his assurances to Moses '**Pharaoh hardened his heart at this time also**'

(6) Exodus 9:7 after the plague of death on Egypt's livestock '**the heart of Pharaoh became hard, and he did not let the people go**'

Then, and only from then God is seen to step in as regards Pharaoh's heart: **(1)** Exodus 9:12 After the plague of boils that broke out in sores on man and beast '**the LORD hardened** [heb. *chazaq* to strengthen, help, fortify] **the heart of Pharaoh**'

So after Pharaoh had (himself) **6** times a hard heart of his own making and once all the support of the magicians had gone (Exodus 9:11) the Lord is then spoken of strengthening Pharaoh's own resolve to not let the people go. And once the Egyptian people were beginning to believe Moses and the Lord (Exodus 9:20) this hardening by God occurred a further **6** times.

(2) Exodus 9:35-10:1 after the plague of hail and fire '**the heart of Pharaoh was hard . . . for I have hardened his heart . . .**'

(3) Exodus 10:20 after the plague of locusts '**But the LORD hardened Pharaoh's heart, and he did not let the children of Israel go**'

(4) Exodus 10:27 after the plague of darkness '**But the LORD hardened Pharaoh's heart, and he would not let them go**'

(5) Exodus 11:10 after the impending death of the firstborn '**the LORD hardened Pharaoh's heart, and he did not let the children of Israel go out of his land**' This is more of a blanket statement to the preceding 4 times since Pharaoh let the people go after the death of the firstborn. So really the next event is:

(5) Exodus 14:8 after Pharaoh had let the children of Israel go, he decided to pursue them because '**the LORD hardened the heart of Pharaoh king of Egypt, and he pursued the children of Israel**'

(6) Exodus 14:17 Despite the pillar of cloud put in their way and the seeing of the divide of the waters of the sea, Pharaoh chased after the children of Israel on the now dry land right to their own deaths, because '**And I indeed will harden the hearts of the Egyptians, and they shall follow them. So I will gain honour over Pharaoh and over all his army, his chariots, and his horsemen**'

So Pharaoh hardened his own heart without outside intervention for **6** times prior to the Lord then *maintaining it that way* a further **6** times. So this is not something that can be said to have occurred against Pharaoh's own will and desire from the start. This then shows again the modus operandi for God in hardening, just as we saw earlier the modus operandi for God having mercy on an individual. Not forgetting God's prime purpose, in the hardening here is to do with, making a Name for Himself on earth.

Without the allusion and context looked at, it 'appears' God is unfair and unjust which is why Paul says God has mercy on whom he will and he hardens whom he wills. Why does he find fault? Who has resisted his will?

And Paul replies God can do what He wants out of the same lump of clay make one to honour and another for dishonour – But PLEASE NOTE on expanding on that premise Paul is careful with his words lest the reader think, as has been supposed, that without any say so, an individual has no part in the choosing of God to bring someone to honour or dishonour.

Having shown by allusion to the context (the source) of his quotes that God can do what He wants with people's lives for His purposes in the nations, Paul now makes this more plain and explicit by his explanation of the next argument for God being sovereign. Paul argues for God clearly by illustrating that He is a potter and we are clay and in His purposes in the nations God can do what He wants with our lives. However, Paul goes on to explain clearly that this action of God involves the state of man's heart in their lifetime.

Paul does not leave the illustration of the potter and the clay in its own in the mind of the reader. He goes on to use two separate and very different Greek verbs to explain the making of one lump of clay into honour and another into dishonour. This is how he does this:

Please read Romans 9: 20-23

3. The Potter and the Clay

Having mentioned Pharaoh and reiterated God will have mercy on whom He wills and then adding whom

He wills he hardens, Paul then thinks of an objection, as he often does in his writings. Earlier in his letter he had proposed the foolish idea that '**we continue in sin that grace may abound**' (Romans 6:1) and then promptly pulls it apart. So here also he brings a foolish remark which he then refutes:

> You will say to me then, 'Why does He still find fault? For who has resisted His will? *Romans 9:19*

This is an objection possible only by someone who reacts without seeing the context behind Paul's earlier statements and quotes. Paul refutes in this fashion:

> But indeed, O man, who are you to reply against God? [my paraphrase follows:] Can it be that the formed shall say to the former, why did you make me like this? Or, the potter with power over the clay, isn't he out of the same lump capable of making either an honourable vessel or alternatively one to dishonour? *Romans 9:20-21 JM*

And then, he adds a very important connected passage which shows both,

1. God's purpose and,
2. His Modus Operandi (verses 20-21 are not to be treated separately from verses 22-23):

> . . . if God, wanting to show *His* wrath and to make His power known [e.g. as mentioned above, due

to His desire to **(1.)** make a name for Himself amongst the nations on earth],[and now, **(2.)** His method of operation:] endured with much long-suffering [a lot of patience] the vessels of wrath prepared for destruction, and that He might make known the riches of His glory on the vessels of mercy, which He had prepared beforehand for glory...   *Romans 9:22-23*

There is a contrast here between vessels of mercy and vessels of wrath.

It is of significant and vital note that one is afore prepared that way *proetoimasen* and the other is fitted/adjusted *katertismena*: One in advance to mercy, the other by other means to destruction. It is also interesting to take another step back and look at what God had said to Moses in the midst of the discourse mentioned earlier. Let's recap.

Prior to God saying He will have mercy on whom He will have mercy, but after His statement that the soul that sins is culpable, God had said to Moses (Exodus 33:5): that if He were to be in the camp of the people of Israel He could in one move 'wipe them out' (due to his anger). Now Moses had already interceded and God for His name's sake, that the riches of His glory be known, His name lifted high, He had mercy on earth with the remainder of the people.

And yet, none of them that sinned were let off (Exodus 32:34b – I will visit their sin upon them) and God could not do this now for His name would be made low if He did that (as Moses argues in Exodus 32:12 as we saw). So instead, He did it later (during the 40 years in the wilderness). So God's Name was glorified and his power known by the use of Pharaoh's hard heart which he (Pharaoh) himself had made fit for destruction, God strengthened it further in that way for His purpose. But his heart was never afore prepared for that by God: there is no warrant for this in the Greek text.

Now it is also seen, that of the same lump of Israel some received mercy right to the end: e.g. Caleb and Joshua (Numbers 14:30) due to their faith, whilst others of the same lump only for a time received mercy (up to 40 years), but in the end wrath in having shown themselves 'fit' for destruction after '**much long-suffering**'. The time lag proved a testimony to God's Name.

The illustration Paul used of a people or individuals, compared to clay in God's hand, was not new to the Jewish mind, or someone familiar with the scripture to Israel, and they could easily recognise an allusion to Jeremiah where God says:

> 'O house of Israel, can I not do with you as this potter?' says the LORD. 'Look, as the clay *is* in the potter's hand, so *are* you in My hand, O house of Israel!'   *Jeremiah 18:6*

The Lord then says if you (Israel) turn from your evil ways I will relent of disaster I thought to bring on you, but if you do evil in my sight when I had planned good on you, I will relent of doing that. This makes clear the cause and effect prevalent throughout scripture which Romans 9 alludes to and supports clearly as soon as the context is examined; it has no backing for unconditional predestination of individuals as far as salvation is concerned. We are all 'afore prepared' *proetoimasen* for good works, but as we refuse this call, we make ourselves 'fit' (for destruction) and are then 'prepared' *katertismena* for dishonour. The prodigal who does not return becomes 'fit' for another purpose.

Finally

Paul ends this chapter by moving away from this illustration which served to show that '**not all Israel who *are* of Israel**' (Romans 9:6) and not all are children of Abraham that are from his seed: i.e. out of the same lump some, after much longsuffering, will be destroyed; while some, as a part of *all* afore prepared, will receive mercy due only to righteousness by (of) faith (Romans 9:30). And this is not just for Israelites who are faithful. Which is Paul's point and reason for the illustration/s all the way through: it is those with faith '***whoever believes on Him***' (Romans 9:33) who are then obtainers of mercy, as opposed to others from the same lump. It is not just faithful Israelites, but it is also faithful Gentiles.

So although as a reader you may be born a Gentile just like me, let us take courage, I have just shown that of the lump of Israel only those with faith are relevant, and so are we if we have faith; our natural birth does not matter as far as heaven is concerned.

This is why Paul carries on to then show from Scripture that God foresaw and spoke of the righteous amongst the Gentiles (Romans 9:25-26), then a few more about Israel in the same fashion (Romans 9:27-29), culminating in Paul's finale: the one who trusts in the Lord shall not be put to shame (thus showing nothing in him fit for destruction).

In other words, **YOU TOO CAN BE A CHILD OF PROMISE**

(Romans 9:8 in context seen with Galatians 4:28).

Now we, brethren, as Isaac *was*, are children of promise.   *Galatians 4:28*

So what is Romans 9 about?

Paul starts by sharing how he feels about Israel as a nation, his own people, in the knowledge that they are not all in Christ Jesus (Romans 8:39-9:3).

As a nation they are valuable and he lists his reasons why (Romans 9:4-5).

Then he says they are not all Israel who are of Israel. There is a spiritual Israel – the children of promise – and there is a physical Israel (Romans 9:6). The physical Israel came about by God's election process as discussed above. This is the Romans 9:7-23 Section, started by: they also not all children who are the seed of Abraham. No one can be in doubt that this nation was picked by God. This is a work of unconditional predestination and can not be denied (Romans 9:7on).

But the word of God about unbelief has not failed. Not all Israel who are of Israel. Even though no reader can dispute God's choice and election of Israel as a nation, only by faith can any in Israel be saved, and be part of the spiritual Israel, children of promise (Romans 9:24, 30).

But you too can be a child of promise even if you are a Gentile. You can become a part of the spiritual Israel – become a true child of Abraham. (Romans 9:24-29).

It is those He calls who are saved. Those called from the physical nation of Israel and those called from the other nations (Romans 9:24). And how this calling occurs Paul explained in Romans 8:28-30, in context: those who love God in their heart of hearts are called by God to be part of His Bride, the Spiritual Israel. Due to the faith seen by God in their heart: it is '*whoever believes on Him*' (Romans9:33).

So, let's take a look at this call mentioned in Romans 8:28 and the conditional predestination Paul teaches.

ELEVEN

ROMANS 8:28 IN CONTEXT

> But we know that to the ones loving God He
> works together all into good, for they are the ones
> called according to a displayed intent.
>
> *Romans 8:28 J. R. More*

This is how I translate this Verse. The commonly
found translation for this passage is as follows:

> And we know that all things work together for good
> to those who love God, to those who are the called
> according to *His* purpose. *Romans 8:28*

Here we see an added word '***His***', and this addition
implies a meaning in the text, or clearly gives a
slant not warranted by the context. I need therefore to
demonstrate the context.

It is of note that the Greek of this Verse gives
no room grammatically for adding *His* in front of

'purpose', irrespective of the context. Just as mentioned in chapter 5 this addition serves an extra-biblical purpose and puts in question the intellectual honesty of the translator at the outset.

I aim also to show that the idea of 'purpose' alone does not give full benefit to the Greek word *prothesis* from which it is translated. Its use for the 'shewbread' in the Septuagint reveals that any 'purpose' or 'intent' is a revealed or seen one: it is 'a showing' of that – A showing of that purpose or intent. I have placed the research on this within the 1st appendix.

The context and the grammar of verse 28 point to a display of intent or purpose seen by God in the life of the individual.

The Context

So what is this context?

The earliest Greek extant manuscripts of the New Testament do not have paragraph or verse distinctions. All the words in these early manuscripts are written without any space between them, without accents, and without punctuation, let alone any chapter divisions. Chapters were added in the 13th century and verses in the 16th. In fact, these early extant copies are written throughout in capital letters. This can make a context arbitrary. It is therefore important to ensure a good grasp of what comes before and after a passage before one attempts to interpret that passage with any degree of accuracy. For the purpose of this commentary on Romans 8:28 I wish to begin the context at verse 17.

Verse 17

> and if children, then heirs — heirs of God and joint heirs with Christ, if indeed we suffer with *Him*, that we may also be glorified together.

As I said a context can be arbitrary.

Here we begin to see a mention of suffering and it is this starting point which I feel best helps to picture a good working context for understanding Romans 8:28. An allusion to the fact that when we are children of God we experience suffering with Christ: Rejection by the world, by those who hold to unrighteousness, lies, etc causes the believer to suffer 'in fellowship' with Christ, just as He suffered. Here adding '*Him*' is appropriate since it refers back to Christ and fits within the Grammar and immediate sense. The suffering mentioned helps to identify us as children of God and thus joint heirs with Christ so that later we may also be glorified with Him.

Verse 18

> For I consider that the suffering of this present time are not worthy *to be compared* with the glory which shall be revealed in us.

Paul then goes on with this train of thought about suffering in verse 18 and I wish to follow through from here all the way onto the passage in question. In mentioning the sufferings of this present time, Paul encourages his reader to look beyond that, to the time when the glory experienced will be far greater and in fact everlasting. The present suffering is only short lived, the time eternal instead will be glorious indeed, and that glory will then be revealed in the believers themselves. As Paul says elsewhere we will be transformed from '**glory to glory**' (2 Corinthians 3:18). Believers will be transformed into a wholly different state of existence.

Verse 19

> For the earnest expectation of the creation eagerly waits for the revealing of the sons of God.

With this revelation of the sons of God in mind Paul then says in verse 19 that the Creation is in fact waiting for this. More than that he says, it can't (really) wait for it, it earnestly and eagerly expects its realisation.

Verses 20-22

> For the creation was subjected to futility, not willingly, but because of Him who subjected *it* in hope; because the creation itself also will be delivered from the bondage of corruption [*decay* – in margin]

> into the glorious liberty of the children of God. For
> we know that the whole creation groans and labours
> with birth pangs together until now.

He then explains himself further in verses 20 to 21. It is as if to prevent an allusion that the Creation as a whole should be believed to have a personality of its own. After all, it is normal to expect people with feelings to eagerly wait for something. He is here then clarifying what he means about the Creation eagerly waiting for the revelation of the sons of God. 'For' – because – Creation was subjected to in-utility, profitless-ness, lack of fulfilment, futility (the older English sense of: vanity). But he says, this subjection is not without hope, because of this bondage it awaits deliverance from it. Man was the crowning glory of Creation. Following the making of all things God said it was good (Genesis 1:25). Following the making of man on top of all that, God said it was very good (Genesis 1:31). Before sin entered the world there was freedom and fulfilment for the whole of Creation. Death, sin, corruption have all caused futility and imbalance in the eco-system of the world. So the Creation awaits deliverance from the bondage of corruption – it's 'suffering' – which will occur at the same time as the children of God also enter into their full glorious liberty.

We know this is true, he says in verse 22 because it is evident that the whole Creation groans and labours under this load even now. The New King James

Version has it '**groans and labours with birth pangs**'. The sighs and groans of the present state of Creation are a witness to the corruption under which it is in bondage. Whether it is earthquakes, volcanic eruptions, tidal waves, tornadoes and extremes of cold and heat these are all signs of the imbalances set in motion as a result of the subjection mentioned. Before the Flood, there may have been no climate allowing for seasons as we now know them and no rain. Also many of the divisions of mountain ranges, rivers, split continents, etc, did not exist: These having been formed during the Flood. All ongoing elements of the subjection of the Creation, due to the corruption and of one of the first judgments upon that: So the Creation groans and waits for the release to come.

Verse 23

> And not only *they*, but we also who have the firstfruits of the Spirit, even we ourselves groan within ourselves, eagerly waiting for the adoption, the redemption of our body.

And not just Creation eagerly waits Paul says, but we also as humans groan within ourselves in our bodies. We await the full redemption to come to which we as believers have a foretaste by the Spirit within us. We long for the adoption to be completed involving the release of our bodies from the common subjection shared with Creation. In this verse, Paul transfers the

118

mention of groaning to the type also experienced by believers and that to one which is within themselves.

Having mentioned suffering, he shows that we are not alone in suffering: Creation suffers too. Just as we suffer Creation also 'suffers'.

Having mentioned a groaning and a waiting, he says that Creation also is not alone in this inner groaning and hope: there is a longing inside of believers too. Just as Creation groans we also 'groan' within ourselves and hope for the release.

Verses 24-25

> For we were saved in this hope, but hope that is seen is not hope; for why does one still hope for what he sees? But if we hope for what we do not see, *then* we eagerly wait for *it* with perseverance.

Because indeed, we were saved in hope: Hope was part of the package of the salvation we as believers entered into. In verses 24 and 25 Paul expounds the virtue of hope itself. It is of value since there would be no need for hope if we had all the promise of release fulfilled totally in us now.

Paul mentions how 'hope' is something held without reference to sight: you don't hope for something you already have, since you already see it. By saying this he encourages his reader to persevere in eagerly awaiting what they hope for (e.g. full salvation). Without being able to see presently what they are hoping for, he encourages them to hold on to this hope.

Verses 26-27

> Likewise the Spirit also helps in our weaknesses. For we do not know what we should pray for as we ought, but the Spirit Himself makes intercession for us with groanings which cannot be uttered. Now He who searches the hearts knows what the mind of the Spirit *is*, because He makes intercession for the saints according to *the will of* God.

Then he says 'likewise', that is to say 'in this same manner' where you do not see what you hope for, 'the Spirit also helps in our weaknesses': in the same way, involving what you do not see (but hope for) being worked out, the Spirit helps in the things we are unable to express, but things we nevertheless desire and long for in our hearts.

This is possible, Paul goes on to say (verses 26 and 27), because God searches the hearts and (due to this searching) He knows what is hoped for in the heart, expressed here as 'the mind of the spirit'. This phrase is equally linked to God in the next few words as it is to the individual in the preceding ones. So in conjunction with the desire of the heart and God's own, 'according to God' the Spirit who sees (the desire in the individual's heart) makes intercession: And that with inexpressible groaning. Paul goes on about groaning to identify the Spirit as also groaning, and that on our behalf. He says the Spirit can do this by reason of the view of the heart He witnesses to (having searched it).

Paul extends comfort in the fact that even though we yearn, but do not know how to express in prayer the longings and groaning we have, He who searches the heart, He knows. It is with this knowledge of what is seen in the heart which enables God (the Spirit who makes intercession) to pray in line with both what is God's desire and the desire in the heart. It is a synergy of wills. The display in view of what is clearly longed for within the heart of the individual, calls on God to meet its longing according to God (in line with His will – which is to be conformed to the image of His Son: verse 29). I believe this is what is meant by Jesus when He says that '**those who hunger and thirst for righteousness . . . shall be filled**' and '**whoever has, to him more will be given**' (Matthew 5:6 and 13:12).

The hunger and thirst in view – the faith in righteousness present – seen by God within the heart, but not altogether recognised and expressed outwardly (by the individual), is a prayer to God to enable the person further to be fulfilled in that particular desire. Although prayers cannot be expressed in words uttered, because we do not know how, God knows how and does this on our behalf as a direct result of the hope in the heart visible to Him: The heart display.

Romans 8:28

It is here that we then come face to face with verse 28. As seen above the verse tells us,

> But we know that to the ones loving God He works together all into good, for they are the ones called according to a displayed intent.
>
> *Romans 8:28 J. R. More*

Paul is here saying what God does as a result of the praying that has been going on. He works together all into good. And this is the next phase of thought which he expands upon in verses 29 and 30. But, he has left us with a clear link to the previous discussion that has been going on. He tells us that it is according to a displayed intent that God works all into good, even to those (who are) loving God.

And what displayed intent is Paul talking about?

What presentation or, setting forth?

It is the loving of God, the desire for righteousness within the heart of the individual, as shown by the preceding verses. The text does not imply another kind of intent, nor that of another person's, being in view: God is not shown us as the (sole) driving force. In verse 28, the displayed intent is placed in apposition to the loving of God. I explain apposition along with my translation at the end of this chapter.

It is the individual loving God who is the one whose heart is observed. This is the evidence of the text. God's desire and purpose mentioned in the next verse '*to be* **conformed to the image of His Son**' comes into play as a result of intercession made on behalf of the heart of love viewed. Paul does not mention it explicitly until then.

Verses 29-30

> For whom He foreknew, He also predestined *to be* conformed to the image of His Son, that He might be the firstborn among many brethren. Moreover whom He predestined, these He also called; whom He called, these He also justified; and whom He justified, these He also glorified.

In verses 29 to 30 Paul explains how this working by God of all together into good comes about. Following a foreknowledge, God predestines or arranges a 'setting up' of the individual.

It is significant that this knowledge, in context involving the knowledge of the Spirit of God after seeing the heart (verse 27) – this knowledge occurs thereby within the lifetime of the individual. There is no implication that the knowledge occurred before the person's life. Equally it is important to notice that it is explicit that the foreknowledge occurs prior to 'a predestination', not the other way around. In the clear language order of the text the predestination occurs as a direct result of the knowledge gained. And predestined to what?

Predestined: to become like the Son of God. Paul here returns to his starting point of being sons of

God and joint heirs with Christ. And he goes on in verse 30 to expand further upon this planning that occurs, this working together of all into good. He says the setting up being planned, a calling occurs in accordance with that plan. A good illustration of this involves Paul's own testimony.

Paul was 'set up by God' on the road to Damascus where he was confronted with his 'call' (Acts 9:1-22). Prior to that, though living in ignorance (1 Timothy 1:13 – just like mentioned above he could not see consciously to pray properly). His heart was nevertheless altogether established for God and loving Him: we know this because he had always '**lived in all good conscience before God**' even when persecuting Christians (Acts 23:1). God who knew his heart 'purpose' (portrayal/display), and as He could see this, He then worked all into good by setting Paul up to be 'called' on the road to Damascus (in spite of his having been Gk: 'a chief sinner' – literally (word for word) in the Greek: '. . . **Jesus He came into the world sinners to save, of whom first I am, I**' 1 Timothy 1:15). As Paul responded to this call, he was justified by God due to the confession of faith in his life now realised fully.

And those God justifies, these He also glorifies, and that at the glorious appearing of our Lord and Saviour Jesus Christ (but let's not forget the need for perseverance – Romans 11:22).

Here we have indeed come full circle, for Paul having begun talking about the future glory to look for as a hope to hold onto in spite of present suffering, he now ends this whole section of his writing with the understanding that those who have been justified will indeed be glorified. Hallelujah!

Romans 8:17-30 is therefore a valuable passage context to enable understanding of the conditional predestination God works in the life of individuals to enable their full salvation.

The Early Church Fathers

Furthermore we have the early Church Fathers who attest to this meaning and this translation. In their commentary on the book of Romans, William Sanday and Arthur Headlam say,

> . . . the great mass of the Greek commentators take **"kata prothesin"** to mean 'in accordance with the man's own proairesis or free act of choice' . . .

A Critical and Exegetical Commentary on the Epistle to the Romans by William Sanday and Arthur C. Headlam Page 216 of the 5th Edition T. & T. Clark

They then mention some of these, namely Theophilus (of Antioch – 2nd century), Oecumenius, and others by abbriv. Euthym. and -Zig. C.E.B Cranfield in his *Commentary on Romans* (also T & T Clark) also adds Origen (c185-254), John Chrysostom (347-407) and Theodoret (d. 466).

All these early writers (except for Theodoret) of course predate Augustine of Hippo who is the beginning of the doctrine in the Church that contains the idea God's purpose alone is in view. See my earlier chapter *The Early Church Fathers and Predestination*. Conditional predestination was the understanding of the early Church Fathers until Augustine: for the first 400 years of the Church's history there is no record of unconditional predestination as a teaching, only conditional.

It is to the Church's loss that during the Reformation period, begun in the 16th century, Augustine's teaching was popularised by writers like John Calvin and the understanding of Romans 8:28-30 has been greatly affected since.

The Translation

I have added dashes to help follow the direct translation and an asterisk (*) at the 'punctuation' break of the Greek Text 'used'.

Romans 8:28 Greek

> Oidamen-de – hoti – tois - agapòsin – ton – theon – panta[2] – sunergei[1] – eis - agathon, * tois[2] - kata[4] - prothesin[5] – klétois[3] - ousin[1]

> But we know – that – (to/for) the ones – loving – (the) - God – all[2] – He works (together)[1] – into - good, * (to/for) the ones[1/2] – according to[4] – a setting forth[5] – called[3] – they are[1].

But we know that to the ones loving God He works together all into good, for they are the ones called according to a displayed intent.

Romans 8:28 J. R. More

Another suitable rendering is,

So we know that He works together all *things* into good for the ones loving God, for they are the ones called according to a displayed intent.

Romans 8:28 J. R. More

NOTES TO THE TRANSLATION

panta = 'all' is the direct object of the verb since it is in the Accusative case. For *all* to 'work together', it needs to be the subject of the verb. *Pas* is the Nominative case (the subject) of the word 'all'. In this passage it is found in the Accusative case.

eis = into

tois = the definite article in the plural dative case: to/for the [ones].

'sunergei' = he/she/it works is third person singular (if it was 'all' [things] that worked it would be in the 3rd person plural: i.e. they work: *sunergousin*).

Kata followed by *prothesin*: which is the word *prothesis* in the Accusative case, denotes *kata* here means 'according to'. If it were in the Genitive *kata* would mean 'against'. There are a number of prepositions in Greek which have 2 meanings and the one relevant is seen by the case in which the following word is found. The nearest we have in English to a change to a word to show a grammatical 'case' is when we add " 's " to mean the Genitive understanding of belonging to or, offspring of. So that "The boy's toy" shows that the toy belongs to the boy: One of the few remaining changes to words to show such connections in English.

There is no Greek word for 'things' so it is not inappropriate for this to be added by English translators. A most regular translation of the passage is as follows:

> And we know that all things work together for good to those who love God, to those who are the called according to *His* purpose.   *Romans 8:28 NKJV*

However as can be seen by the grammatical case of *panta* 'all', it is more accurate to read all is worked together by God than all works together. Also it will be seen that the translator has placed the word *His* before 'purpose' in italics. This is to show they have added it and is not from the Greek text. As can be seen from the context explanation above, it is unwarranted and indeed contradicts the flow of the text. The translation of *prothesis* into 'purpose' is also in question as I expand upon and explain in Appendix 1. It is more appropriate here to understand it as a 'displayed intent' (which in itself is a way of expressing a person's "purpose" but a seen one).

Apposition

An apposition is the placing of things side by side. Grammatically this means a placing of words syntactically parallel with one another. In Romans 8:28 we find "**tois agapòsin**" – the ones loving God – in apposition with "**tois . . . klétois**" – the ones called. They are linked in this way syntactically. This means that even when there are words in between, they are linked in complimentary meaning. This is so here because the phrase "**panta sunergei eis agathon**" – He works all [things] together into good – are 'in between' the 2 phrases in apposition. Greek as a language involves the relationship between words in a sentence more than the order in which they are found. This is important. In English "a man speaks to an angel" means something different than "an angel speaks to a man", but every word is identical. Their form has not changed. The order determines the meaning. In Greek this is not so. The form of the words determines the relationship with the other words in the sentence. I mentioned this already in the notes above in regards to *panta* and *sunergei*.

The reason I highlight this is that *prothesin* is part of the phrase '**tois kata prothesin klétois**'. This is in apposition to '**tois agapòsin ton theon**'. And, since this means they complement each other, they are thereby an expansion or explanation of each other. In other words the *prothesin*, the 'purpose' which I have translated as 'a setting forth' or, 'a displayed intent' is no other than the loving of God. And as explained in the commentary this is a reference to the 'unknown' loving of God within the individual. The display in view is the loving of God within the individual: this is the prayer seen by the Spirit which makes God work all things together into good.

Paul puts extra emphasis on the apposition by making "**they are**" last. To the Greek reader it comes out like this:

> So we know that He works together all *things* into good for the ones loving God, for the ones called according to a displayed intent they are.
>
> *Romans 8:28 J. R. More*

Conclusion

The Verses leading up to Romans 8:28 describe a longing within the individual which is not matched by understanding in the mind. This prevents effective prayer or seeking to satisfy this longing. God who searches the heart however sees this display within and the Spirit intercedes on behalf of the seeker (within). God as a result arranges all things into good: He predestines the individual believer to be 'set up' to a calling. In response to that calling, the individual's confession releases justification which at the Lord's return leads to glorification. The addition in Romans 8:28 of *His* in front of purpose is thereby a diversion from the context of the passage. This suggests God's purpose is in view, whilst in fact the individual's heart display of love for God is what Paul is describing. The grammatical apposition in the Greek text is direct testimony to such an understanding, let alone the context. This is attested by the early Church Fathers and makes good sense of the whole text and complements things Jesus said as reported in the gospels:

It is those who '**hunger and thirst for righteousness**' who '**shall be filled**' (Matthew 5:6).

> But we know that to the ones loving God He works together all into good, for they are the ones called according to a displayed intent.
>
> *Romans 8:28 J. R. More*

TWELVE

THE APOSTLES PAUL AND JUDAS

———

The apostles Paul and Judas Iscariot are opposites in the New Testament. One is known as a faithful teacher whilst the other as a betrayer, but they both started out in a different role to the one they are now known. Judas was perceived as a follower of Jesus and Paul as an enemy of Jesus. It is this observation which makes each of them useful as illustrations of unconditional predestination (allegedly). I wish to show the bible reveals them as not having changed in their heart or root purpose.

In unconditional predestination teaching Paul is said to have been transformed and changed into someone he himself was not desirous to be: it is understood by implication that Paul never wanted or asked for this. Hence in this way he is seen as a useful illustrator of God's unconditional choice to salvation. Conversely Judas is understood as not having use of free-will for if he had, as is understood, how could he have fulfilled his 'role' as betrayer: would that not have put God's plans or foresight in jeopardy? He is thus used as a pointer to the total inability of man especially in the realm of free-will.

These understood considerations, believed in this way, make both these characters worthy of attention and I aim to show the biblical record testifies that the way both these men turned out was in fact the direction they were inclined and wanted to go in the first place: the true state of their heart's desire from the beginning did not change throughout their life as it is recorded.

The Apostle Judas Iscariot

Judas Iscariot: was he a child of God and fell, or was he not a true child of God from the beginning?

Did Jesus pick him, as one of his apostles in the knowledge that his heart was not honestly towards God, or that it was, but that he would turn away from God?

The scripture tells us that Jesus knew what was in man and therefore had no need that anyone should testify of man (to Him)[1]. This is not to say he knew everything about every heart of man, but that Jesus was familiar with every kind of heart and how to discern them. We know this does not refer to any supposed omniscience on the part of the Son of God (on earth) since he would then never have asked '**Who touched Me?**' as he did[2].

So Jesus was conscious of how to recognise all men[3] in that he was familiar with the signs and evidence for what was in them[4]. John the writer of the gospel who tells us this also wrote some letters. In one of these he says '. . . **even now many antichrists have come . . . They went out from us, but they were not of us, for if they had been of us, they would have continued with us; but *they went out* that they might be made manifest, that none of them were of us**'[5].

Jesus called Judas Iscariot '**the son of perdition**'[6] and the Antichrist of prophecy is given that name also in 2 Thessalonians 2:3. It is to John also that we are indebted for the record of the fruit of Judas Iscariot's life: following expensive ointment having been poured on the feet of Jesus, Judas complained that this could have been sold for three hundred denarii and given to the poor[7]. However, John then tells us: '**this he** [Judas Iscariot] **said, not that he cared for the poor, but because he was a thief, and had the money box; and he used to take what was put in it**'.

Now we know that Jesus said he who was unjust in little was unjust in much[8]. And since he had good vision as to recognise what came out of the heart, I believe it was on purpose, that the scripture might be fulfilled that, after some time with a number of followers, Jesus picked 12 men and one of them he already knew the heart was not toward God: Judas Iscariot[9].

> . . . Jesus knew from the beginning who they were who did not believe, and who would betray Him.
>
> *John 6:64*

Luke mentions that after continuing all night to God in prayer Jesus chose 12 whom he also named apostles[10]. But John also tells us that Jesus lost none of those whom the Father had given him[11]: Because as he states in his letter, Judas was not in his heart of hearts 'one of them'.

The fruit of Judas' life is told us by John in the midst of the context that Jesus as The Logos, is the Light that gives light to every man who comes into the world[12]. Every person who takes hold of this light by believing in it (no outside assistance is mentioned in the text at this stage whatsoever) is then given the right (after taking hold of the light for themselves assistance is then given) to become a child of God[13]. It is these whom the Father draws to Jesus[14]. Because just as Jesus explained by quoting from the prophets in the following verse '**"they shall all be taught by God." Therefore everyone who has heard and learned from the Father comes to me**' (John 6:45). Here we find Jesus explaining what he has just stated earlier. God is in the business of teaching about spiritual truths and those who learn these things come to Jesus. "*All*" are taught, but only those who receive [take hold of for themselves] this teaching, are thus then drawn to Jesus. They are the ones mentioned in John 1:12 as receiving Him who are *then* given the right to become children of God.

But, as John put it in his letter Judas Iscariot had never been one of them as evidenced by his practise of evil (1 John 2:18-19). This practise Jesus tells us in

John 3:20 is evidence that someone does not believe in the light (i.e. the Name of the only begotten Son of God[15] and is not therefore born of God [i.e. again] – see *The Meaning of Born Again* in my book *Will there be Non-Christians in heaven?*

So Judas Iscariot was a recognised 'plant' by Jesus and he allowed it that the scripture might be fulfilled and be a valuable lesson to the 11. Nevertheless, Jesus loved Judas (even called him 'friend' as he was kissed/betrayed), but was not going to impose upon him, His own real desire for him (i.e. that he might be saved – e.g. 1 Timothy 2:4). The works of Jesus was testimony enough etc... But Judas '**loved darkness rather than light, because** [his] **. . . deeds were evil**'[16]. Just as Abraham said to the rich man in hell, they have Moses and the prophets as a witness and even if one should rise from the dead they would still not believe[17] – as was indeed confirmed by the Pharisees and the Jews against Jesus who knew of Lazarus' resurrection (the other Lazarus), yet did not repent[18]. They had already chosen to love darkness and were by this not given authority to see (cause and effect) lest they should repent (due to inherent capacity to do so as shown by the constant parable purpose '**That "*. . . hearing they may hear and not understand; lest they should turn, and their sins should be forgiven them*"**'[19]. Jesus recognised it was Judas Iscariot's choice: to love darkness – and this is why I believe he was picked to fulfil the scripture.

Paul the Apostle

Paul mentions in the book of Romans that he had not known sin except for the law[20]; if it was not for the law he would be ignorant of sin. He also mentions that there is 'law' which is written in the heart[21]. This internal law, when violated, results in conscience accusing the offender[22]. Thus Paul advocates for doing what you know to be right. He is also aware that you can do wrong without knowing that what you are doing is wrong[23]: by doing an act in ignorance that it is in itself not right.

Paul's own persecution of the first Christians is a clear case in point. Paul did this in a time of ignorance: without knowledge that this was wrong. To him, at that point in time, not to persecute the Christians was to allow the name of his God and his religion to be defiled. His conscience as it was at that point would not be clear if he did not persecute Christians. The law and thus the knowledge of wrongdoing in this activity, this was not present in his heart and mind: Which is why he can tell us after having become a Christian, and an apostle of Christ at that, his conscience has been clear before God and man (up) to that day.

> . . . I have lived in all good conscience before God
> until this day. *Acts 23:1*

There was no envy in his heart out of which he persecuted Christ unlike the way the Pharisees and religious leaders had done[24]. Which is why Jesus said to him '*it is* **hard for you . . .**'[25] He was already God's man for this was his honest purpose '**before God**'. He had not violated any law that he knew of concerning what was wrong. The moment that he learned and was no longer ignorant concerning the fact that persecuting Christians was in fact attacking the very Lord he was trying to serve, he was no longer free by conscience to do this act against the law. The law he had now learned. Of course by using the word law I use the same expression that Paul uses, but in modern day thinking the word truth may be more appropriate. The moment Paul had gained the truth that acts against Christians was acts against God his conscience would no longer be clear were he to go on fighting them.

However, until that truth was real to him, his belief was that not to persecute Christians was to allow tainting of the religion of his fathers. The God of the Torah was blasphemed by the followers of 'the way'. So his heart which was zealous for God would not permit him to rest whilst this 'heresy' was propagated.

Paul said that '**where there is no law** *there is* **no transgression**'[26] and that '**sin is not imputed** [taken account of] **when there is no law**'[27]. So it can be seen that until Paul learned the truth that his persecuting acts were wrong, until he understood transgression was involved, though he was committing sin, God who knew his heart motive was not holding it against him. That sin was not taken account of until there was knowledge of the truth that it was wrong.

Paul's heart was so much for his God that his heart's prayer was to be able to follow God. God saw this and he thereby arranged,

1. Paul to go away from Jerusalem by his trip to Damascus and away from those persecuting Christ with the wrong motives
2. Paul to be challenged on the road to Damascus and thus,
3. Paul to be set free and healed to follow God more fully just as his heart desired[28].

> For whoever has, to him more will be given, and he will have abundance; but whoever does not have, even what he has will be taken away from him.
>
> *Matthew 13:12*

Notes

1 John 2:24-25
2 Luke 8:45
3 John 2:24
4 John 2:25, 3:20-21
5 1 John 2:18-19
6 John 17:12
7 John 12:1-8
8 Luke 16:10
9 John 6:64
10 Luke 6:12-16
11 John 18:9
12 John 1:9
13 John 1:12
14 John 6:44a
15 John 3:18
16 John 3:19
17 Luke 16:19-31
18 John 11:1-44 then 45-47 and 12:9-11
19 Mark 4:12 quoting Isaiah 6:9, Matthew 13:13-15
20 Romans 7:7 & 3:20
21 Romans 2:15
22 Romans 2:14-15
23 1 Timothy 1:13
24 Matthew 27:18
25 Acts 9:5
26 Romans 4:15
27 Romans 5:13
28 See the previous chapter on *Romans 8:28 in Context*.

THIRTEEN

I BELIEVE IN PREDESTINATION

—

Predestination and salvation

Yes, I believe in predestination. As the preceding two chapters show Paul was predestined to a call on the Damascus road, following God seeing his heart loving Him. '**For whom He foreknew, He also predestined . . . whom He predestined, these He also called**'[1]. As expounded in *Romans 8:28 in Context* God foreknew Paul's heart as loving Him during his lifetime before this trip to Damascus. He therefore then predestined Paul to be on that road and near to Damascus and away from Jerusalem. This was away from those persecuting Christians out of different motives than Paul. Jesus then called Paul on the road and this led to his conversion and repentance and thereby his justification '**whom He called, these He also justified**'[2]. Conditional predestination is taught

143

by Paul. As regards salvation this is what the bible reveals.

Predestination and particular jobs

There is also predestination that involves particular jobs that God requires to be done on earth and with these tasks in mind God is seen to speak about these as done by particular individuals before they are born or soon after. The first we read of prophetically is Jesus right back in Genesis 3 as the Seed that would bruise the Serpent's head[3] then, more visibly in the immediate text is Noah who would bring about a relief to humanity in regards to the toil involved in acquiring sustenance[4]. Following the universal Flood, the Lord permitted man now to eat meat and removed the curse on the ground[5]. The curse removed then meant there was relief from the persistent toil involved in obtaining sustenance before the Flood. Noah's name means 'Rest'. Joseph was predestined to rule in Egypt[6]. Moses was appointed to deliver Israel from Egypt[7]. Pharaoh was picked to enable God to show his power on earth[8]. And many more: Cyrus to release the captives of Israel to rebuild the temple[9]. Jeremiah was picked to prophesy[10]. John the Baptist was to precede Jesus' coming[11]. Jesus from the beginning is the Lamb of God who takes away the sin of the world[12].

However Jesus said plainly:

Many are called, but few eklektos. *Matthew 20:16*

I have demonstrated that this word *eklektos* is predominantly used in the bible Jesus quoted to mean: quality, tops, best, fit for purpose. This I mention further in *The meaning of Elect* – chapter 16, and provide all the research for this in Appendix 2. So that Jesus said,

> Many are called, but few are fit for it.
>
> *Matthew 20:16 JM*

God chose Saul to be the first king over Israel[13]. He did not prove fit for the call however. So God rejected Saul as king and then called David to carry on this important task[14]. There were no prophetic words about David until Saul was rejected as king[15]. But, throughout there are tasks lined up for those within the groups they are in. Whether the Righteous[16] or, the Wicked[17].

You choose which group you are in. But let's slow down and spend a moment with the Ephesians passage referred to.

> . . . He chose us in Him before the foundation of the world, that we should be holy and without blame before Him in love, having predestined us to adoption as sons by Jesus Christ to Himself, according to the good pleasure of His will . . . we are His workmanship, created in Christ Jesus for good works, which God prepared beforehand that we should walk in them. *Ephesians 1:4-5, 2:10*

Here we read of good works prepared beforehand for those in Christ to walk in. Tasks prepared to be done by those in this group. But instantly, if you have been brought up to believe in unconditional predestination this passage reads differently. This is why I wish to spend a moment to address that.

Paul said that:

> All Scripture *is* given by inspiration of God . . .
> *2 Timothy 3:16*

Paul was writing there about the Old Testament. Now anything God breathed is inspired in the original language (cf. *eklektos*) and is also accurate. By this I am saying that to appreciate a text one must be careful not to read into it what it does not explicitly say. But that it can also be very precise.

Now Peter mentioned Paul's own writings when he said,

> . . . our beloved brother Paul . . . has written . . . his epistles . . . which those . . . unstable twist . . . also the rest of the Scriptures.   *2 Peter 3:15-16*

Thus we can see that Paul's words above in Ephesians are also understood as God breathed. Now, if we look carefully at this famous Ephesians passage we will see that the thinking of Paul never touches upon an individual believer in this passage, but instead the Body of believers. This can be quickly seen by a perusal of the pronouns used: us, us, we, us, us, we, us, us, we, we . . . (Specifically, Ephesians 1:3 '**us**'; 1:4 '**us**'; '**we**'; 1:5 '**us**'; 1:6 '**us**'; 1:7 '**we**'; 1:8 '**us**'; 1:9 '**us**'; 1:11 '**we**'; 1:12 '**we**').

The group is in view; not the individuals within. This is important. Paul makes clear it is those in Christ who are involved. He makes clear elsewhere both how we are in this group in Romans 8:28 and that we can leave in Romans 11:22. Yes, perseverance is dependent on continued faithfulness on our part. Paul said,

> Therefore consider the goodness and severity of God: on those who fell, severity; but toward you, goodness, if you continue in *His* goodness. Otherwise you also will be cut off. *Romans 11:22*

His being an added word by the translator just like in Romans 8:28 and is equally not required. In any event by then adding '**you also will be cut off**', Paul removes any doubt that just as the unbelieving Jews were cut off, so those who do not continue in goodness will also be. So being in the group of the righteous – in Christ – is not pre-determined or permanent if one chose to deny goodness[18].

But which group you are in predisposes you to enter into the inheritance of good works if among the righteous or, to be used like Pharaoh was for example if persistently wicked.

Predestination of Jesus is the only absolute individual type that can justifiably come near to being named unconditional. But this is only because He is all of God in a human body[19] and thereby unchanging[20]. No one else is.

As Peter put it on the day of Pentecost '[Jesus was] **delivered by the determined counsel and foreknowledge of God**'[21] and in one of his letters '**He indeed was foreordained before the foundation of the world**'[22]. John writes of him as '**the Lamb slain from the foundation of the world**'[23] which is no wonder that hundreds of prophecies were given about him. These have been fulfilled in his first coming and many more remain to be carried out during his subsequent return.

Predestination in the bible

Conditional predestination to salvation of individuals, predestination to particular callings and prepared good works are what the bible reveals. Those whom God foreknows are predestined (set up, as Paul was on the road to Damascus) to a call. But as we saw this knowledge is after heart activity of the individual is seen by the God who searches the heart. Predestination to particular tasks is also dependent on the individual remaining steadfast and faithful or else the responsibility is passed on to another. The extent of God's knowledge therefore warrants to be given particular attention. I begin this in the next chapter.

Elmer Darnall a previous Principal of Christian Life College in London – now 'promoted', as the Salvation Army saying goes – used to say, election (the other word used for 'predestination') is something like this: "God's got a vote; the Devil's got a vote; you choose which way the election goes!"

NOTES

1 Romans 8:29-30
2 Romans 8:30
3 Genesis 3:15 and Galatians 3:16
4 Genesis 5:29
5 Genesis 9:3 and Genesis 8:21
6 Genesis 37:1-11
7 Exodus 3 though I could not find prophecy or words of this in his early days, but see Genesis 50:24
8 Exodus 9:16 cf. chapter 10
9 Isaiah 44:28
10 Jeremiah 1:5
11 Luke 1:13-17
12 John 1:29 and Revelation 13:8
13 1 Samuel 10:24 and 2 Samuel 21:6
14 1 Samuel 16:1-13
15 1 Samuel 13:13-14
16 Ephesians 2:10
17 Proverbs 16:4, Isaiah 66:4, 2 Thessalonians 2:11-12
18 Romans 11:22 if you doubt this understanding read and meditate on Ezekiel 18:19-32
19 1 Timothy 3:16 'God was manifested in the flesh' and Colossians 1:19
20 Hebrews 13:8
21 Acts 2:23
22 1 Peter 1:20
23 Revelation 13:8

FOURTEEN

EVIL AND GOD'S KNOWLEDGE

———

When we read about God in the following terms,

> . . . of Him and through Him and to Him *are* all
> things . . . *Romans 11:36*

And,

> . . . All things were created through Him and for
> Him. And He is before all things, and in Him all
> things consist. *Colossians 1:16-17*

And,

> You are worthy, O Lord, to receive glory and honour
> and power; for You created all things, and by Your
> will they exist and were created. *Revelation 4:11*

It is easy to think these are all encompassing statements. Nothing appears excluded. Certainly, '**all things**' would appear to give that idea.

However, scripture explains scripture and one thing is not included in '**all things**': evil.

Evil is excluded from this. We know this by reading that,

> . . . God is light and in Him is no darkness at all.
> *1 John 1:5*

In writing this John is not alluding to photons or the lack of them. Physical light is not at issue here. What is being spoken of is evil – darkness in that sense – has no place in God. Indeed it is also written that,

> . . . You *are* not a God who takes pleasure in wickedness, nor shall evil dwell with You. *Psalm 5:4*

What does all this say about God?
It says that God is not acquainted with evil and is unable to produce it or, think of it or, plan it. With no evil in God a question or more then arises.

Where did evil come from? How did it begin?

And, perhaps more relevant to our true understanding of God when did this begin?

Why when?

Well, the determination of when evil began in the midst of the existence of all things is a pointer to the extent of God's knowledge. If evil has no part in

God, then evil's first appearance indicates a moment where God is seen to learn something outside of His experience. Since evil is something outside of God's pure character, evil's existence is the beginning of new information for God. The extent of God's knowledge therefore has limits.

And since the bible is the only source of information for Christian believers to effectively trust and use to learn about God due to its inherent inspiration by the Spirit of God in its production, is there a moment shown us where God is 1st seen to discover evil? A moment when evil is 1st 'found' in a being created by God?

Yes, I think so.

We read in Ezekiel of an angelic being which was (who was?) created perfect.

But then, we read, how he was found with iniquity. We are shown that there existed the anointed cherub who was perfect, as shown by the words:

> You *were* the anointed cherub who covers; I established you; you were on the holy mountain of God; you walked back and forth in the midst of fiery stones. You *were* perfect in your ways from the day you were created . . .   *Ezekiel 28:14-15*

We then read,

> . . . Till iniquity was found in you.   *Ezekiel 28:15*

This is probably a record of the first thing God ever learned. The discovery of evil in a being God had created perfect.

Since God is not acquainted with evil, due to in Him being '**no darkness at all**', it is inconceivable that He knew of this evil before it occurred.

Of course He knew of the possibility of it, but He had no way of knowing how it would occur or when, since this entails knowing and understanding the mechanics of evil: being acquainted with it. To think or believe He did know is to say He was familiar with evil and even had planned it into being. Which is why the scripture has '**till iniquity was found in you**'. It was found: it was something discovered and learned about: By God Himself.

After all, it happened to someone who had been created perfect. God did not implant evil in that person or planned it.

Other pointers

This is why in mentioning grievous evils which fallen Israel was committing – in this instance, the sacrifice of children by fire – God says:

> . . . they have also built the high places of Baal, to burn their sons with fire *for* burnt offerings to Baal, which I did not command or speak, nor did it come into My mind . . . *Jeremiah 19:5*

This specifically tells us of something which had not come into God's mind. This evil had never occurred to God, since in Him there is '**no darkness at all**': He is not acquainted with evil. The act of sacrificing children by fire had not occurred to God. This is the testimony of scripture.

The way created beings have turned from God and followed evil is something which God has been learning about since it began. Once it has occurred and a pattern has established, God is seen to put into place obstacles or limitations to limit its existence or its effects for the future. This is true of God's dealings with men from Genesis onwards.

Examples

An immediate example is the curse on the ground (Genesis 3:17-19) which was removed after the Flood, since this event brought in better and more suited limitations: New rivers and mountain ranges having been formed, etc. The removal of that curse also came with an expansion of the reason for it '**I will never again curse the ground for man's sake, although the imagination of man's heart *is* evil from his youth**' (Genesis 8:21).

The wickedness of man, allowed for by his passivity, was restricted by the curse on the ground. He had to keep busy to obtain food, thus the cause for man's part in allowing the eating of the forbidden fruit, and any further evil was restricted: due to man's inherent passivity. Passivity in Adam allowed Eve's deception to be put in practise. Passivity if given time to allow evil, permits the practise of the evil imagination based in pride. The curse on the ground meant severely restricted time to permit passivity to influence negatively.

After the Flood new restrictions were in place. These were added to at the tower of Babel by new languages causing division amongst the wicked (Genesis 11). As government amongst men became a feature even more restrictions on growth of wickedness became effective (Romans 13:1-7). The rules of life truly changed by the means of the Flood: Vegetation alone was no longer a fully viable support for mankind. This meant God now gives permission to eat meat (Genesis 9:3). That is quite a change alone after 16 centuries of existence. And the use of multiple languages to confuse wickedness in a group was not needed for those many centuries whilst everyone was busy working to overcome the effects of the curse on the ground before the Flood. I have added at the end of this chapter answers to objections to the thought that the curse on the ground was removed.

Had God known at the beginning, the growth of wickedness as He did by the time of the Flood, would He not have placed those new restrictions at the start and not provide a new set of rules for life? The Flood itself would have been unnecessary. Could this be some of what was explained when Jesus **'preached to the spirits in prison'** – to those who had lived in Noah's day (1 Peter 3:19-20)?

Since God never decreed or planned for evil's existence due to no facet of His Being having darkness, then it is only as a pragmatic response to evil's existence that He makes plans to redeem those under its influence, to limit its existence and effects and, to allow it on occasion to bring things about for long term good. This is all good stuff and has no indicator or implication of evil in God Himself. The use of what is there – an evil practise by someone for example - without being a part of that practise, is not an indicator of evil in God. Here is an example.

God is seen to use a lying spirit to make some people fall who had already chosen against the truth (1 Kings 22:20-23).

> . . . The LORD has put a lying spirit in the mouth of all these prophets of yours, and the LORD has declared disaster against you.   *1 Kings 22:23*

Again in The New Testament we read of those who,

> . . . because they did not receive the love of the truth, that they might be saved . . . for this reason God will send them strong delusion, that they should believe the lie . . .   *2 Thessalonians 2:10-11*

There is a clear cause and effect here. Those who have chosen to believe a lie will have this enforced for them. As Jesus said '**For whoever has, to him more will be given, and he will have abundance; but whoever does not have, even what he has will be**

taken away from him.' (Matthew 13:12). Those who have no desire to believe and follow righteousness will see their ability to do so removed or extinguished. As shown by the above 2 passages this removal is done by reinforcing the delusions chosen. This is permitted evil and is used for God's ultimate purposes in the nations as shown by the example of causing the people to fall in battle in the Kings passage and to create a powerbase for the antichrist in the Thessalonians passage.

Another good example can be seen with Pharaoh in the time of Moses whose heart God hardened. This 'strengthening' of Pharaoh's heart occurred following his own desire to be against God's people (see chapter 10 where I outline in detail with regards to Romans 9 how Pharaoh first hardened his heart 6 times and then the Lord 'strengthened' it in that state a further 6 times). This hardening of Pharaoh's heart was done in order for God to show His power in the nations.

This is not God planning evil in the first place, but making use of its existence to His own ends. For God to plan evil and be the cause of its existence is to contradict scripture. This can be seen further when Jesus said,

> Every kingdom divided against itself is brought to desolation, and every city or house divided against itself will not stand. *Matthew 12:25*

Every kingdom Jesus said and since,

> The face of the LORD *is* against those who do evil . . .
>
> *Psalm 34:16*

God's kingdom is not for the evil doer. If God planned for evil, He too would be evil and divided against Himself.

The Devil wants us to believe God is to blame for the existence of evil. This is why his first recorded words involve '**Has God indeed said . . . ?**' (Genesis 3:1), that is to say, 'God cannot be trusted – He is not pure – He is not full of truth'. This was his first words to Eve as he began his work of deceiving her. Jesus did well to call Satan the father of lies:

> . . . he is a liar and the father of it.   *John 8:44*

Whereas the testimony of God is:

> God *is* not a man, that He should lie . . .
>
> *Numbers 23:19*

It is a deceit pure and simple to conceive of God as the originator of evil – something He never decreed, planned for or executed. He cannot for '**God is light and in Him is no darkness at all**'. He is not acquainted with it. For Him to plan it, He must understand and be acquainted with it. He must conceive of it and that out of Himself: a complete blasphemy!

This is therefore a positive pointer to the limitation of God's knowledge.

For example, it helps us to understand the act of choosing Saul as king, as no mistake on His part. For the evil that Saul turned to, was not in God's mind. It explains why His reaction to the rebellion of Saul is to honestly say via Samuel the prophet:

> . . . the LORD would have established your kingdom over Israel forever. But now your kingdom shall not continue . . . *1 Samuel 13:13-14*

Up to that point there is no mention in the Bible of David, the next king to be. The next sentence is the first:

> The LORD has sought for Himself a man after His own heart, and the LORD has commanded him *to be* commander over His people, because you have not kept what the LORD commanded you.
> *1 Samuel 13:14*

King Saul rebelled in a manner not foreseen by God. To think otherwise is to bring into doubt the statement that God '**would have established your** [Saul's] **kingdom over Israel for ever**'. God had picked out Saul to be the first king and we see from Samuel's words that God had planned for his kingdom to be over Israel for ever. It is easy to see, for example, how Saul's son Jonathan would have made a good king. But, it was not to be. How true are Jesus words,

> Many are called, but few *are* fit for it. [few are quality] *Matthew 20:16; 22:14 J.R. More*

160

Please Note again: the usual translation of '. . . few *are* chosen' does not tally with the most common use of the word *eklektos* in the Septuagint. The 'fat' cows coming out of the Nile in Pharaoh's dream as interpreted by Joseph were *eklektos* cows – quality meat; 'young men': guys in their prime; 'Choice' silver; The 'pleasant' land; 'tall' trees, etc. . . The common emphasis is quality not 'a selection'. The Septuagint is the 200 or so year old translation of the Old Testament into Greek which Jesus and the apostles used and quoted. This being the common use of the word *eklektos* and known by Jesus when he said the above statement, it makes this a perfectly valid and the most appropriate meaning/translation. This is also true wherever 'elect' and 'chosen' has been translated elsewhere in the New Testament from the word *eklektos*. So when you read of 'elect angels' think 'the good ones'. The 'elect' or 'chosen' think 'the saints' or, the 'quality guys'. For a full account of my research of this word in the Septuagint see the 2nd Appendix.

This limit upon God's knowledge tallies with His testing the hearts in order to judge accordingly.

Who does the judging?

God

So, it is for His purpose in judging that He tests. To know what is in the hearts. It is in order that He knows the true motives for the acts of men.

> I, the LORD, search the heart, *I* test the mind, even to
> give every man according to his ways, *and* according
> to the fruit of his doings. *Jeremiah 17:10*

> . . . the LORD your God led you all the way these forty
> years in the wilderness, to humble you *and* test you,
> to know what *was* in your heart, whether you would
> keep His commandments or not. *Deuteronomy 8:2*

A clear example for the purpose of God to know is
told us in King Hezekiah's life where,

> . . . God withdrew from him, in order to test him,
> that He might know all *that was* in his heart.
> *2 Chronicles 32:31*

The inspiration of the text makes clear the cause and
effect. God withdrew, to test Hezekiah, so that God
might know by observation all that was in the king's
heart. This also makes sense of the Lord's words after
testing Abraham with Isaac his only son from Sarah,

> . . . for now I know that you fear God, since you have
> not withheld your son, your only *son*, from Me.
> *Genesis 22:12*

How did evil first come about?

It is evident from Genesis 3 that Satan, also known as
the Serpent, the Dragon, and the Devil (Revelation
12:9) was already a doer of evil before man. When he
tempted Eve as mentioned above, his first words were

to allude to God being evil Himself. Apart from this we do not know when it was that Satan fell. The anointed cherub mentioned in Ezekiel as being perfect until iniquity was found in him, may be and is likely to be a reference to Satan, but apart from the evil in both there is no other clear link. Jesus said:

> I saw Satan fall like lightning from heaven.
>
> *Luke 10:18*

This tells us that Satan was in heaven and had a role there and also that he fell. We are aware that he is not alone:

> . . . the dragon and his angels fought . . .
>
> *Revelation 12:7*

So, how did these originally good creations of God fall?

They are shown in scripture as sentient beings and have a freedom to choose what to do. This can be seen by the reaction of angels when communicating with man:

> . . . I fell down to worship before the feet of the angel who showed me these things. Then he said to me, "See *that you do* not *do that* . . . Worship God."
>
> *Revelation 22:8-9*

The good angels know to receive worship is to take the place of God: idolatry.

This is not just an emotive reaction, but a conscious recognition that to worship any other than God is wrong. Idolatry is encouraged by demons (also known as devils e.g. KJV) for when Paul writes about offerings to idols he says:

> . . . the things which the Gentiles sacrifice they sacrifice to demons and not to God . . .
>
> *1 Corinthians 10:20*

Demons are fallen angels who desire to receive worship. They chose, at some point, to stop giving God the praise and wanted it for themselves. They wanted to live independent of God. This is when evil first took place. For evil is doing anything apart from God: outside of His character. Outside of His created order. This was possible because any free being – one that is not a robot – is able to choose for themselves the direction of their lives.

The workings of this evil act by an angel of desiring worship for himself, of thinking himself better or greater than he is – pride – are all evil. The mechanics of doing this evil are not a part of God's Being since '**God is light and in Him is no darkness at all**'. There is no pride in God. He resists them:

> *God resists the proud, but gives grace to the humble.* *James 4:6*

This makes the first act of doing this evil a thing discovered and learned by God, since He is not familiar

164

with the mechanics of it. To say otherwise is to imply God's appreciation of evil and acquaintance of it. Even to say He planned or decreed it.

Since worship is befitting for God alone,

> I *am* the LORD, that *is* My name; and My glory I will not give to another, nor My praise to graven images.
>
> *Isaiah 42:8*

Then, He has had no part in any plan to have anyone receive worship other than Himself. God has therefore never made any plan to have angels to share His worship. The turning to evil of the angel is not known by Him until it occurred.

A question to the reader:

Do you believe God planned or decreed someone other than Himself to receive worship?

God cannot at the same time decree something to happen in eternity (past) and then, declare something in opposition to that. He cannot agree and disagree at the same time. That is confusion. He is not divided against Himself. Sin is not something He desires or plans into being:

> Let no one say when he is tempted, 'I am tempted by God'; for God cannot be tempted by evil, nor does He Himself tempt anyone.
>
> *James 1:13*

165

What does God know?

An awful lot: He knows all that is knowable.

God knows the amount of hair on all our heads, the very number of molecules in the universe are not hidden from Him. He knows infinitely more than all other beings put together, because He created them all. It does not mean everything though, as we have seen. Evil and the desire for it, has caused God to search out the motives of man. This is so that His judgments are based on truth.

We also see the knowledge of the future is limited to the plans He ensures comes about. That is how prophecy operates.

> Remember the former things of old, for I *am* God, and *there is* no other; *I am* God, and *there is* none like Me, declaring the end from the beginning, and from ancient times *things* that are not *yet* done, saying 'My counsel shall stand, and I will do all My pleasure'
> *Isaiah 46:9-10*

What He purposes to do, He ensures comes about. This tells us that His knowledge of the future is based on what He plans to do and carries out taking into account the existence of evil and what He permits and limits of it. It is not therefore a knowledge based on some view 'outside of time' as if it were there already, but on His appreciation of the present and His involvement to cause the events to occur in the set future time.

> . . . Indeed I have spoken *it*; I will also bring it to pass. I have purposed *it*; I will also do it.
>
> *Isaiah 46:11*

So, how does one view a passage like Ephesians:

> . . . He chose us in Him before the foundation of the world . . . having predestined us to adoption as sons by Jesus Christ to Himself, according to the good pleasure of His will . . . being predestined according to the purpose of Him who works all things according to the counsel of His will . . .   *Ephesians 1:4, 5, 11*

Predestination is a reality which cannot be denied. There is the predestination of nations and that of individuals. The nation of Israel is predestined to be the home of the Messiah who is Jesus Himself who will return and rule from there. He is predestined to this role. Nations are set to rise and fall according to prophecy. Things which the Lord will ensure occur. There is a grouping known as the Church which is also predestined and just as with the nations individuals are able to join the Church. When reading Ephesians it is of note, as outlined in the previous chapter, that the group is in view by the multitude of pronouns used throughout: we, us, you and your (in the plural). In Old Testament language the generic terms used for the 2 main groups of people on earth were '**the righteous**' and '**the wicked**'.

> Let the wicked forsake his way, and the unrighteous man his thoughts; let him return to the LORD, and He will have mercy on him; and to our God, for He will abundantly pardon. *Isaiah 55:7*

> 'Do I have any pleasure at all that the wicked should die?' says the Lord GOD, '*and* not that he should turn from his ways and live? *Ezekiel 18:23*

> Far be it from You to do such a thing as this, to slay the righteous with the wicked . . . *Genesis 18:25*

> . . . the LORD knows the way of the righteous . . .
> *Psalm 1:6*

> A little that a righteous man has *is* better than the riches of many wicked. *Psalm 37:16*

The examples are plentiful. Two groups were in view and all you need to do to be part of '**the righteous**' as the first quote shows is to repent and turn to God. Equally you could choose to be part of '**the wicked**':

> When a righteous *man* turns away from his righteousness, commits iniquity, and dies in it, it is because of the iniquity which he has done that he dies. *Ezekiel 18:26*

This is true also of the New Testament. He who repents and turns to Jesus becomes a part of the Church: The Body of Christ. It is the Church as a whole that is predestined to good works and adoption. If you are found in Him then you are known as righteous. If you rebel and sin you are not.

Objections to the curse removal addressed

To help concrete the interpretation that God removed the curse on the ground in Genesis 8:21 by removing some possible objections I offer the following:

> . . . and Jehovah saith unto His heart, 'I continue not to disesteem any more the ground because of man, though the imagination of the heart of man *is* evil from his youth . . .'
>
> *Genesis 8:21 Young's Literal Translation*
> *of the Holy Bible*

This verse as translated by Robert Young helps to show that by '**I will never again curse the ground**' as translated in the NKJV, the meaning is more to do with 'I do not allow the curse to continue' than 'I will not do it a second time'. The latter understanding of course has the problem also of suggesting that doing a curse a second time is something perhaps necessary for God to do: i.e. cursing once by God is insufficient.

Some would say that a curse by God on someone is irreversible nor is a blessing from God irreversible. This would tally with the truth that a calling on someone's life does not change or a gift from God is not taken away as per Paul's words:

> For the gifts and the calling of God *are* irrevocable.
>
> *Romans 11:29*

In the KJV this is translated as '**the gifts and calling of God *are* without repentance**'.

Which some have read to mean that a man need not repent to still have these, but the context refers to God not changing His mind. It is His repentance that is in view. So to remove such misunderstanding more modern versions have used the word 'irrevocable'. So this verse would support the view that a curse or a blessing from God on someone is irreversible.

However it is not a person or even a living entity that has been cursed in Genesis 3:17 and removed in Genesis 8:21, it is the ground. It is not someone, but an object for a purpose. This purpose is mentioned in both passages and it is that purpose for which it served that the curse was put there, and then removed. Something different was put in place to 'take care' of the purpose.

Now some will note that Robert Young does not translate the word 'curse' in his translation. This is because the word *Qalal* has been used in the Hebrew as opposed to the word *Arar* in the earlier mention.

There are two main Hebrew words for 'curse', ARAR (62; also used for 7 other words a total of 7 times) and QALAL (41; also used for 27 other words a total of 40 times).

This shows that for both *arar* and *qalal* the prime use is for 'curse'.

Other words for 'curse' in Hebrew are ALAH (19), BARAK (4), CHEREM (7), MEERAH (5), NAQAB (6), QABAB (7), QELALAH (31), SHEBUAH (1), TAALAH (1).

Words used for 'curse' in Greek in the New Testament

Anathematidzò (3); Ara (1); Epikataratos (3); Kakologeò (2); Katanathema (1); Katanathematidzò (1); Katara (6); Kataraomai (6)

This is helpful in that the Greek translation of the Hebrew Old Testament translates both *Arar* and *Qalal* with the same root word in Greek *katara* in Genesis 3:17 and 8:21. Showing that for those translators the 2 passages in question meant a curse in the same way.

Now Quoting from both Hebrew words translated as curse in the case of Naaman it can be seen that they can also mean the same thing.

Translated from Qalal

> . . . they hired against you Balaam the son of Beor from Pethor of Mesopotamia , to curse you.
> *Deuteronomy 23:4*

> . . . king of Moab, arose to make war against Israel, and sent and called Balaam the son of Beor to curse you.
> *Joshua 24:9*

> . . . they had not met the children of Israel with bread and water, but hired Balaam against them to

171

curse them. However, our God turned the curse into
a blessing. *Nehemiah 13:2*

Translated from Arar

And Balaam . . . took up his oracle and said . . .
Blessed *is* he who blesses you, and cursed *is* he who
curses you. *Numbers 24:2-3, 9*

Therefore please come at once, curse this people for
me, for they *are* too mighty for me. Perhaps I shall
be able to defeat them and drive them out of the
land, for I know that he whom you bless *is* blessed,
and he whom you curse is cursed. *Numbers 22:6*

So, even though there is more of an emphasis in *qalal*
to a curse as in swearing or demeaning someone's
name, it can be readily seen it is used effectively in the
stronger sense that *arar* mostly gives, that of a spiritual
pronouncement with power.

Also it must not be forgotten to suggest God
just merely speaks evil or denigrating (despising)
the ground in Genesis 8:21 whilst He had cursed it
(proper) in Genesis 3:17 is to say what? God doesn't
like the ground? He despises it?

No, but instead it makes sense that in Genesis 8:21
just as in the examples just given of Balaam, cursing
using the word *qalal* is equivalent and indistinguishable
as *arar* within these contexts.

A final note about The Curse and curses in the bible

The world of doctrine and theology has made much use of 'The Curse' as it relates to salvation. The bible alone mentions many curses. Some explicitly like the one in question upon the ground. Some implicitly or inferred by the feeling that something bad is in itself a curse: these can include sin, death, the groans of creation (as mentioned by Paul in Romans 8:22), etcetera. One specific curse removed – as discussed – does not infer the removal of any other real, inferred or imagined 'curse'.

Objection of anthropomorphic language

There are those who argue that the passages referring to a lack of knowledge on God's part are illustrative by using anthropomorphic language. To God are attributed arms, hands or that he sits. He is mentioned with human emotions: love, hate, jealousy and anger. God is said to whistle, have wings, etc. God is said to be a potter or a shepherd or a father or a husband. The purpose for this language is not to describe the entirety of God, but to address a particular matter in the immediate context in which the mention appears. So that when God is said not to be like men, it is only a reference to lying like men do (Numbers 23:19).

However, when he says now he knows or he tests to know what illustration is this about?

It is a description and a revelation pure and simple to show the real facet of God that he wishes us to know about. No more. The purpose of testing is repeatedly given us to reveal God's need and desire to know something new. I don't wish to argue the revelation given by the inspiration of those passages; I wish to accept them since they do not contradict the rest of Scripture equally read in context. It is dangerous ground to doubt the inspiration of the text and rather to base a view of God on attributes not revealed in Scripture.

FIFTEEN

DOES GOD KNOW EVERYTHING?

———

Some would immediately say:

Well, of course He does, or He wouldn't be God!

Which is fine: this is something which is believed and everyone is free to believe it, but my question really is,

Does The Bible show us the God who inspired its contents as someone who knows everything?

We may feel He does or think so, but if this is not the revelation given to us in scripture it is a belief which is extra biblical and no other doctrine could or should be built upon it. Indeed, the belief that God knows everything about the future some would say is at the root of the idea that He has predestined certain individuals – out of the midst of the many – to be saved; the many that remain have been left as 'un-chosen' and are destined to be lost. This is all very well but again only if sufficient evidence is given from The Word of God as to its reality should this also be believed.

Allow me to show you some clear indicators that, although God knows all that is 'knowable' and this encompasses more than the knowledge of all other beings put together, this knowledge is limited as concerns a range of situations involving the freedom of choice imparted to man.

The alternative, that God knows everything and in particular everything about the future I aim to show is more a recipe for confusion than for the truth as revealed in scripture.

The Omnis

God's knowledge is also termed his omniscience and is one of the three 'omnis'.

Omnipresence (there is no space where God is not present).

Omnipotent (there is nothing He cannot do).

Omniscience (there is nothing He cannot know).

But we don't have to look far to see the limitations of the three Omnis.

God's omnipotence is limited by the fact that he cannot make 1+1=3 and still only have two elements. Equally he cannot make a square out of a circle and still call it a circle: so it is evident that there are limitations to God's omnipotence.

So it is with His omnipresence, God '**fill**[-s] **heaven and earth**' (Jeremiah 23:24) as scripture tells us, but it is evident that until something else were to come into being, God is unable to be present there also. For example He does not (yet) fill the new heavens and the new earth '**which I** [God himself] **will make**' (Isaiah 66:22), because he has not created them yet, so it is evident that there are limits to God's omnipresence.

So it is with God's omniscience, until something becomes a reality in thought or deed it is not something which can be known by God in all circumstances. This is where scripture indicates the limits of God's omniscience: it involves future events which are not part of the foretold plans of his purposes (these are shown to be known about, only due to His determined actions designed to bring these about). The limits revealed range upon the genuine free choices given as – an ability – to mankind within the scope of choices he has been set (allowed).

King Saul

If you have read the previous chapter this is not totally new. This is an expansion and further explanation.

In Israel there was no king until God spoke to Samuel his prophet and directed him to pick out Saul a Benjamite to be their first king. Saul was chosen by God for this role, this post, as king (1 Samuel 10:24, 2 Samuel 21:6):

> . . . Do you see him whom the LORD has chosen . . .
> *1 Samuel 10:24*

> . . . Saul, *whom* the LORD chose . . . 2 Samuel 21:6

After ruling for a while, Saul deliberately rebelled against God and on one such public occasion, Samuel came along and said these words to Saul:

> You have done foolishly. You have not kept the commandment of the LORD your God, which He commanded you. For now the LORD would have established your kingdom over Israel forever. But now your kingdom shall not continue. The LORD has sought for Himself a man after His own heart, and the LORD has commanded him *to be* commander over His people, because you have not kept what the LORD commanded you.   *1 Samuel 13:13-14*

I would like to look at '**the LORD would have established your kingdom over Israel forever. But now your kingdom shall not continue**'.

If the Bible is inspired and profitable for doctrine (2 Timothy 3:16) and God does not lie (Numbers 23:19, Titus 1:2), then I am bound to believe that God would indeed have established Saul's kingdom over Israel for ever.

Now if God knew beforehand that Saul (the king He chose) was going to be a rebel like he became, then it is impossible for Him to have established his kingdom over Israel for ever.

So, either He would have established Saul's kingdom, or, He would not. Since God does not lie, and I believe the above passage is scripture and therefore inspired by God, I can only conclude that

God did not really know beforehand how Saul was going to end up.

For this passage to make full sense, the choice is simple, either God did not fully know beforehand and is telling the truth about the fact that He '**would have established your** [Saul's] **kingdom over Israel for ever**', or, God is not telling the truth: He in fact would not have established Saul's kingdom, in the full advance knowledge that he was going to be rejected.

To my mind it is very plain: I believe God is telling the truth, the scripture is inspired and it makes full sense of God not to know fully the free choices of man until they are made in a range of circumstances. I believe the Bible shows us that there are a limited but real range of things He cannot know until they are chosen: this is not to say He is surprised in any way by these, because to Him, they were already in themselves part of a range of clear probabilities and possibilities (with few exceptions – see Jeremiah 19:5).

If God knew beforehand that Saul was going to rebel in the way he did, He would know that He would not have established Saul's kingdom for ever and what He says, that He '**would have**' is not true. This is why believing God knew everything beforehand is confusion.

It makes sense that God did not know, it makes sense that this passage quoted includes the very first mention in scripture relating to David the '**man after His own heart**' as the next king to be. Prior to that passage there is none. How could there be, since God did not wholly know beforehand this outcome.

Other pointers

In the previous chapter I outlined precise words that explicitly show God testing so He would know something new. It is helpful to remind ourselves: Where God is seen to acquire knowledge: '**now I know**' Genesis 22:12; '**God withdrew from him, in order to test him, that He might know all** *that was* **in his heart**' 2 Chronicles 32:31; '**the LORD your God led you . . . to . . . test you, to know what** *was* **in your heart, whether you would keep His commandments or not**' Deuteronomy 8:2; '**God is testing you to know whether you love the LORD your God with all your heart and with all your soul**' Deuteronomy 13:3.

I also touched on how prophecy operates. By God ensuring that his foretold plans come to pass.

The wicked dying before their time

Another pointer is that we find wicked men – in particular – clearly mentioned as dying before their time.

> . . . the years of the wicked will be shortened.
>
> *Proverbs 10:27*

> Do not be overly wicked, nor be foolish: why should you die before your time? *Ecclesiastes 7:17*

... wicked men ... cut down before their time ...
Job 22:15-16

Bloodthirsty and deceitful men shall not live out half
their days.   *Psalm 55:23*

The fact that God never desires directly anyone to
sin, it is not conceivable within the revealed order of
things that God knows the extent of a life before it is
started in all cases: God's knowledge of future events
is not absolute. To say God knew they were going to
die early is really to say: 'that is the actual extent of
their lifetime', *so* 'that is its full term' – for them – is
not an occasion of dying before 'their time'. You
cannot say they are dying early if that was the time
'they should go'. Is it any wonder that to believe God
knows all things future is confusion?

The whole of unconditional predestination
thinking founders on this point alone.

The pointers are not few to show that there
is a limitation to God's foreknowledge. This strips
away the foundation for the idea that God knows
beforehand all who would be the 'elect' (of course
I refer to 'elect' within that 'thinking'). I believe
God told truthfully to Saul that He '**would have
established . . .** [his] **kingdom over Israel for ever**'
and therefore did not know beforehand that he would
reject Saul. I believe God knows all that is 'knowable'
but this is limited to many true free choices man
makes. Therefore I cannot believe that God has chosen

individuals to be saved over and above others since that would be against His revealed nature and workings in the Bible.

Did God create time?

This question has an important bearing on all the above. It is another pointer.

It makes sense that if God created time, everything that happens in time is wholly known by God. He would then know every detail of the future of individuals before even Creation came about.

It is as if time was a line drawn on a page with a beginning and an end. The present would be represented by a point somewhere along the line (and moving along it), and the future would be the remaining portion of that line. The rest of the page would then represent 'non-time' where God exists and the 'place' from where He could therefore see everything on this line. If this is true then it would indeed make sense that God knows every detail of the future of individuals prior to their existence.

Personally, I would like to believe what God has given as the source for all doctrine and teaching, the Bible. If this idea is valid then, due to the use of it as a foundation to the edifice of so much teaching, it is vital that only from the Bible we gain the evidence for its reality. Does scripture reveal to us the existence of 'non-time', does it mention time as a created 'object', or instead, does it reveal to us that time and God have always been?

There are two basic views of time in relationship to God: one is that He created time and the other is that time has always been with Him. These are mutually exclusive views: both cannot be true at the same time. To know which is true we need to see what evidence there is to support one or the other. If there is any support for one than the other cannot be true. So what kind of evidence do we need to look for? The same is true for God's knowledge: He either knows all future or there are limits to His knowledge. Mutually exclusive views are great in this sense: You only need proof of one to reveal the truth of both.

Passages which refer to God and time
God is shown to experience time differently to us (as to its extent),

> . . . with the Lord one day *is* as a thousand years, and
> a thousand years as one day.   *2 Peter 3:8*

The immediate context of this passage tells us that this occurs within the framework of God's patience and this thinking correlates with Psalm 90:4 where we read in a prayer attributed to Moses,

> . . . a thousand years in Your sight *are* like yesterday
> when it is past . . .   *Psalm 90:4*

Now, if God created time (and thus 'non-time' exists) then, a thousand years would be as a day, *before* the thousand years as well as *during* the thousand years, *not just* '**when it is past**'. Already then we have a pointer to time not being created, but that instead God was with time before The Creation. Verse Two of the same Psalm in fact tells us this very thing,

> Before the mountains were brought forth, or ever You had formed the earth and the world, even from everlasting to everlasting, You *are* God. *Psalm 90:2*

Before creation of the earth this verse tells us that God was present from everlasting to everlasting.

Probably the closest statement we have that God lives within time is:

> For thus says the High and Lofty One Who inhabits eternity . . . *Isaiah 57:15*

There is an immediate problem here however. To some the word 'eternity' renders 'time' meaningless and they are two separate concepts. This may be so in their minds, but only what the scripture declares is worthy of believing first and foremost. In Micah 5:2 we read about the coming of Jesus,

> . . . Whose goings forth *have been* from of old, from everlasting. . . *Micah 5:2*

'**Whose goings forth *have been* from of old, from everlasting**'. The Hebrew for the last words is literally 'from the days of eternity' (as found in many margins):

yomyomowlam = 'daydayeternity' = 'days of eternity'. It makes clear therefore that there were set moments i.e. one after the other, before the world was made and that it is thus nonsense to separate time from eternity (as far as scripture is concerned).

In the Jewish calendar Yom Kippur is an important day: the Day of Atonement. The word *yom* for day is therefore well known. When it is realised that the inspired Word of God has *yomyomowlam*: daydayeternity then it follows that the impression God wishes us to have of time is as an entity which co-exists with Him.

There is of course the simple logic that if God created time then, what did He do before its existence?

He could not have a conversation or, do anything with a beginning and an end. '**Let us . . .**' would be a permanent event. This is nonsense. For if, He was to start something, and then stop it for a moment then all this took a period of time. It has a beginning and an end. There needs to be events one after the other for existence of a person to make any sense at all. It makes no sense of God as a living Being to exist outside of time. To say He is outside of time is confusion in my mind. As we saw from Micah 5:2 the literal Hebrew shows us otherwise: God is very much in time.

We saw above a number of statements which state that individuals as a result of persistent evil have their lives shortened from what length they would have been. There are also those due to their 'free-choices' have their lives lengthened from what it would be.

In other words the evidence is not insignificant for lives of individuals not to have a fixed extent prior to their birth, such that knowledge of this cannot logically be said as complete in God's mind prior to that person's life. If God was outside of time, then by His mere observance of all 'in time' there is no such thing as a life shortened or lengthened. It would be a fixed time: period!

(As our beloved American cousins would say)

> The fear of the LORD prolongs days [Hebrew. addeth], but the years of the wicked will be shortened.
> *Proverbs 10:27*

> For by me [wisdom] your days will be multiplied, and years of life will be added to you. *Proverbs 9:11*

> *'Honour your father and mother,'* which is the first commandment with promise:
> *'that it may be well with you and you may live long on the earth.'* *Ephesians 6:2-3*

A counter argument

Another argument is sometimes expressed that since Genesis 1:1 expresses '**In the beginning God created the heavens and the earth**', the word '**beginning**' implies a beginning for time also. The real question here should be, 'In the beginning' of what?

The context shows in the beginning, at the start of his creating, the first job he did was to make the heavens and the earth. This does not say, or infer that time was created, just that the moment God began creating God started with the heavens and the earth.

Psalm 139
Of course let's not forget Psalm 139.

> For You have formed my inward parts; You have covered me in my mother's womb.
>
> I will praise You, for I am fearfully *and* wonderfully made; marvelous are Your works, and *that* my soul knows very well.
>
> My frame was not hidden from You, when I was made in secret, *and* skillfully wrought in the lowest parts of the earth. Your eyes saw my substance, being yet unformed.
>
> And in Your book they all were written, the days fashioned for me, when *as yet there were* none of them. *Psalm 139:13-16*

This passage especially in the NIV can be seen as useful to the doctrine of unconditional predestination, **'All the days ordained for me were written in your book before one of them came to be.'** (Psalm 139:16 NIV). The idea is that if God has written up all the days of our lives before they existed, then you can't help but see unconditional predestination as a reality. He must thereby also know how long each one of us has got.

The Hebrew literal which can be found in KJV margins has '**what days they should be fashioned**'.

In other words the order in which his body was fashioned was known and understood in detail by God. This is my understanding of this text portion. So that in the KJV we have:

> Thine eyes did see my substance, yet being unperfect; and in thy book all *my members* were written, *which* in continuance were fashioned, when *as yet there was* none of them.   *Psalm 139:16 KJV*

There is in context no appreciation that the days of one's life is known by God in advance, but instead the order in which the parts of the body are knit together in the womb: the days in which *they* should be fashioned (emphasis mine). See also Young's translation.

Conclusion

As we have seen then, there is direct and indirect evidence in scripture to reveal that time has always been and that it was not part of the creation. God can thus be seen to live only within time and that not unlike love, faith and wisdom, time has always been an existent 'entity' prior to the creation.

God's knowledge is seen to be incomplete in regards to the length of time everyone will live their life on earth.

The choices given to man where there is real freedom to a number of alternatives is seen in scripture as points in time where the outcome is unknown beforehand by the God of the bible.

SIXTEEN

THE MEANING OF ELECT

———

The unconditional predestination view is that the elect refers to a group of individuals chosen by God as destined for eternal life. I aim briefly in this chapter to show that the Bible meaning is unlike this thinking. Instead it involves individuals which are part of a group which is special to God and as part of that group identity are known as elect.

The understanding that by elect the Bible emphasis lies in a 'chosen' individual over and above or out of the midst of other similar individuals, I believe is totally flawed. If this were so than in the following verse:

> . . . My elect One *in whom* My soul delights . . .
> *Isaiah 42:1*

A place where Jesus is spoken of in prophecy as the 'Elect One', the meaning would be given that He has been chosen amongst others for the role He plays.

SO YOU THINK YOU'RE CHOSEN?

And since that would invalidate the truth of the Lord Jesus' deity, it is dangerous ground.

Jesus was not picked as one from amongst others equally available. This is the clear logic of believing 'elect' refers to a choice of God. Equally, when the Bible speaks of '**the elect angels**' (1 Timothy 5:21) it does not refer to angels chosen out of the midst of others, but something altogether different. Part of the reason for a misunderstanding of elect has arisen due to the translation of the Greek word *eklektos* in the New Testament. Into English this has been translated as chosen (7) and elect (16). The reader of the New Testament in the first century was familiar with the everyday Greek and the above connotation of 'specially picked' or 'chosen out from others' would not have entered his mind.

There are two pointers for my being able to say this:

1. There is no record of a teaching of 'predestination of individuals' (unconditional) in the early church until Augustine came along. So for about 400 years any such notion was not taught (See chapter 6).
2. The general meaning for the word *eklektos* was not 'chosen' or 'elect'.

And why should a Greek speaker not see such a meaning? Because all 'elect' meant to him was something or someone who is 'special', 'choice' (in that sense). A colloquial English equivalent would be someone who is a real 'brick': Which of course does not mean you can use him or her for building a house!

And how can we know this was the emphasis? Simple, just read it from the Bible the first Christians used known as The Septuagint. The Septuagint, with the reference LXX, is the Greek translation of the Hebrew Old Testament of the Bible. It was carried out c266BC and became the common used Bible for Jesus, the apostles and the first Christians. It is the version found quoted in the New Testament. This is why quotes in the New Testament are often found to differ in detail to the reference in the Old Testament of today's Bible, which was directly translated from the Hebrew. My primary use of it here is to identify the common understanding of the day for the word *eklektos*.

In the Septuagint *eklektos* can be well seen as not meaning any more than a 'special' kind. In Pharaoh's dream, which Joseph interpreted in the book of Genesis, the word is used of the fat cows that came up out of the Nile. This was because they were plump and well built. Like a 'choice' piece of meat from a butcher. They were simply 'elect' in that sense.

Further examples are easy to find. If we look at the words used by translators into English from the Hebrew Old Testament and compare them to the word *eklektos* used in the Greek translation we see that a choice by God was not any primary understanding of the word, but 'special', 'good', 'tops':

N.I.V and A.V. translations of the Hebrew O.T. text followed by the Greek word in the Septuagint

(the 'New Testament Greek' translation of the Hebrew text)

Zechariah 7:14	AV - 'the **pleasant** land'	- eklektén
Zechariah 11:16	AV - 'he shall eat the flesh of the **fat**'	- eklektōn
Haggai 2:7	AV - 'the **desire** of all nations'	- ta eklekta
Habakkuk 1:16	AV - 'their meat **plenteous**' (Margin: **dainty**, **fat**) /NIV '**choicest** food'	- eklekta
Ezekiel 25:9	AV - 'the **glory** of the country'	- eklektén
Ezekiel 27:20	AV - '**precious** clothes'	- eklektōn
Ezekiel 27:24	AV - 'chests of **rich** apparel'	- eklektous
Ezekiel 31:16	AV - '**the choice and best** of Lebanon' NIV '**choicest and best**'	- ta eklekta
Daniel 11:15	AV - 'his **chosen** people' (Margin: the people of his **choices**) NIV 'their **best** troops'	- eklektoi
Jeremiah 22:7	AV - 'thy **choice** cedars' NIV 'your **fine** cedar beams'	- tas eklektas

| Lamentations 5:13/14 | AV - 'the **young men**' [i.e. in their prime] | - eklektoi |
| Ezekiel 17:22 | AV - 'the **highest** branch' NIV 'the **very top** of a' | - eklektōn |

(For the exhaustive examples see Appendix 2)

A Christian is 'choice' or special only because of the righteousness and 'choiceness', the special-ness of Jesus with which he has clothed himself by faith.

It is the righteousness of Jesus that makes a Christian different in God's eyes. Only in this sense is a Christian elect. It is nothing to do with a choice of God of that individual, but an entering into the Body of Christ which is choice (elect) before God [i.e. special]. Which is why a perusal of the pronouns of Ephesians One, the passage 'used' often to credit the idea of an individual's predestination, show that the group, the body is in view and not the individual. I believe to say otherwise is misleading. A brief perusal of the pronouns in the context of this passage shows this well as exampled in chapter 13. I find no evidence for my being able to say that individuals are chosen before the foundation of the world to salvation. Some are shown as chosen for a particular work on earth, but as to salvation what I find is those who are a part of Christ and those who refuse to know Christ i.e. only two distinct groups.

This is not to say as such that the group itself is foreseen (in its entirety) and thus the constituent individuals, but that the existence of the group was foreseen and that God desires all to be part of the Body of Christ. He has prepared for those that love Him many things. And the predestination of Ephesians One is of those as part of the Body of Christ (itself) which was foreseen and these are thus named as elect. Hence the fact that it says '**chose us in Him**' (Ephesians 1:4): it is whilst in him that we are chosen, elect and share in his 'election' – his perfection and righteousness – and that by the operation of our own faith: '**whosoever believeth on him shall not be ashamed**' Romans 9:33 AV.

Please note that under discussion has been the adjective *eklektos* not the verb *eklegò/mai*

SEVENTEEN

WHY I BELIEVE 'UNCONDITIONAL PREDESTINATION' IS ERROR

——

John Calvin is probably the best known advocate of the teaching of unconditional predestination. Due to this supporters of the view are often termed 'Calvinists'. Here are some of the things Calvin taught taken from what is possibly his most famous work: *The Institutes of Christian Religion* which comprises four volumes:

Calvin's Institutes III xxiii 7, 8: Calvin asserts that all men are made liable to eternal death owing to the wonderful counsel of God. God is said to have arranged **'at his own pleasure'** the fall of the first man, and in him the ruin of his posterity. He says that the depravity of man is a result of God's creation and that God had expressly approved what preceded from himself. Further he says **'the first man fell because the Lord deemed it meet that he should fall'.**

This is the most revealing aspect of unconditional predestination because it lays at God's door the responsibility for the fall of man. The fall was the act of the first sin. Calvin is saying that this sin was purposed by God to be carried out. Here we have the root of the tree: the real nature of the beast. Satan has from the beginning given man to believe that God is not true. He has deceived man into believing that God is not all good and perfect. Here the Devil wants us to believe that God who is light has desired, purposed or willed (whichever way you want to put it) for evil – sin – to be carried out. It is a direct attack (though subtle) on the character of God. Scripture is black and white on this issue:

> God is light and in Him is no darkness at all.
>
> *1 John 1:5*

Also as regards God's desire about sin it goes on to say:

> God cannot be tempted by evil, nor does He Himself tempt anyone. But each one is tempted when he is drawn away by his own desires and enticed.
>
> *James 1:13-14*

God neither tempts anyone thus enticing them to sin, nor does He give desires to sin. He that does not lie cannot at the same time ever approve of anyone to sin and equally to hate sin. The thing is, this is at the root of unconditional predestination and is a wholly deceitful defamation of God.

By attempting to reconcile God's sovereignty to the fact of evil in the world and its origin, God is said to initiate evil whilst in reality He is '**light and in Him is no darkness at all**'. God never wants anyone to sin yet this is what Calvin is telling us to believe. It is probably the most fundamental fruit of the doctrine of unconditional predestination, thus revealing its true source.

The Devil who tempted Jesus in the wilderness knows well the scripture but forever uses it in part and out of context[1] and veils the eyes[2] to the balancing portions. This unconditional predestination doctrine is a complete package of deception full of out of context scriptures and ideas foreign to the very nature of God. And they are strung together to make up this false 'doctrine'.

So we are told to believe that God, by eventually rejecting the hypocrites, that in fact '**He never loved them**' in the first place (*The Sovereignty of God* by A W PINK page 54 sixth edition). This flies in the face of:

> '*As* I live,' says the Lord GOD, 'I have no pleasure in the death of the wicked, but that the wicked turn from his way and live . . .   *Ezekiel 33:11*

It is contrary to '**God so loved the world that He gave His only begotten Son**'[3]. Satan constantly works to limit the reality of God's love in the mind of man let alone the work of the cross and the effect of Jesus' blood shed. He hates it. So that limited atonement is a 'natural' product of unconditional election: Jesus is said to have shed his blood just for 'the few' who eventually benefit and God is said to love only these He has chosen. If this were so God is a liar when He says '**I have no pleasure in the death of the wicked**'. Either '**God is light and in Him is no darkness at all**' or, He is not.

Either he loves them or he does not. Ah! But surely anything God desires comes to pass, it is argued. If He wanted everyone to be saved they would be saved: God's will is always done. This is a profound misunderstanding of the nature of God.

God does not impose His will: it is against His nature. So that He never desires sin; He does not will sin. Yet it is everywhere carried out by fallen men and women: wasteful of the gifts God has given. He convicts of sin and commands to repent, but this is resistible by the gift of free-will within every man. To then say they are unable to repent and turn 'of themselves' because God has caused it (by an inscrutable wisdom) that their nature is so depraved they cannot choose for God is to call God a liar. God is said to impart depravity to all so that they cannot help but sin.

This is defamation of the most serious kind and that upon the living God: upon the very Creator of the universe.

Evil, sin, depravation are not a facet of God's being and they never emanated from Him: '**God is light and in Him is no darkness at all**'. He has never decreed that anyone should sin or carry out any form of evil: this never enters His mind.

The honour of God's Name is at stake here.

The enemy is so subtle that he has taught this doctrine[4] very powerfully. The truth is that evil never emanates from God, it never has and it never will in any form or kind; The Error is that God has at some point started the process involving the sin of the first man as planned by Him.

God's love is such that no man is made in any shape or form to do evil by God nor is man forced to do any good by God. The way God is involved in the good in a man's life is by synergy of the two wills in action. The will of God is never for evil so this He resists. For good He is inspiring and encouraging and helps in the process as we will with Him for these things. He cannot by His very nature impose His will upon our will. This is the stumbling-block of those who currently believe in unconditional predestination.

God never enables a man to do something he himself does not will in his very being. Even with many Christians, He is knocking outside the door of their life desiring to come in[5]. And even to them also it is written **'Draw near to God and He will draw near to you'**[6]. God has self control and He exercises it such that His gentleness[7] does not allow Him to coerce, drive, impel against someone's will[8]. Instead He convicts, persuades, corners etc... But if someone remains persistently unrepentant, then God releases them to this[9].

This is the testimony of scripture. God loves all, desires none to sin, has paid the price for all, but only those who will believe will be saved.

It is not God's intent that any should sin, nor is it any part His intent that any should be lost. If He desires none to sin it follows that He desires none to be lost: If all were not sinning as God desires, then all would be saved as God desires. This is a natural progression from the fact that '**God is light and in Him is no darkness at all**'. As an outworking of His perfect Nature God does not choose some to be saved and leave others to perish: unconditional election of individuals to salvation is error.

And here as elsewhere in this text 'all' means 'all', there is no part dark just as there is no one wished lost and no one unpaid for. 'All' is never exclusive in this setting. Unless of course as with other scriptures, as a believer in unconditional predestination, you wish to twist its meaning as Satan does and limit the 'all' of '**God is light and in Him is no darkness at all**' to mean of course this must exclude the beginning of evil in the world. Do you?

> *Do not be deceived, my beloved brethren*. Every good gift and every perfect gift is from above, and comes down from the Father of lights, with whom there is no variation or shadow of turning.
>
> *James 1:16-17 (italics mine)*

NOTES

1 Matthew 4:1-11
2 2 Corinthians 11:3
3 John 3:16 – see also Chapter 1
4 1 Timothy 4:1-2
5 Revelation 3:18-20
6 James 4:7-8
7 Galatians 5:22-23
8 1 Corinthians 13:4-7, James 3:17, Luke 13:34
9 Romans 1:25-26, 2 Thessalonians 2:11-12 See my chapter on *The Wicked* in my book *Will there be Non-Christians in heaven?*

EIGHTEEN

WHY GOD HATES GRACE THEOLOGY

——

Does God really hate bad teachings?

Yes, Jesus is on record as saying:

> . . . the doctrine of the Nicolaitans, which thing
> I hate. *Revelation 2:15*

We also know that all the bad things Job's friends said
about God they were expected to repent of:

> . . . the LORD said to Eliphaz the Temanite, 'My wrath
> is aroused against you and your two friends, for you
> have not spoken of Me *what is* right, as My servant
> Job *has* . . .' *Job 42:7*

This was because what they said about God did not
match His character. They were not true about Him.

So why should God hate 'Grace Theology'?
Indeed, what is it?

It is the belief system, the doctrine which claims that worthless sinners, dead and depraved in character are chosen and redeemed by God unto salvation. These are called acts of grace where God is said in His mercy to snatch from eternal death unmerciful and unworthy individuals.

The problem with false doctrine is that there are elements of truth. Here the truth involves God's mercy and that He does freely give salvation to imperfect individuals. Satan always makes use of ½ truths to capture his victims into a set of errors: Just as he quoted scripture at Jesus when he tested Him in the desert (Matthew 4:1-11).

The lies involve what is opposite to what God has expressly said in His Word: the Bible. This is what Jesus said which can be seen to differ from what has just been described as 'Grace Theology':

> Blessed *are* those who hunger and thirst for righteousness, for they shall be filled. Blessed *are* the merciful, for they shall obtain mercy. *Matthew 5:6-7*

How is this different from Grace Theology? (GT)

Reformed Theology, Unconditional Predestination, Calvinism, all being titles of the same set of doctrines, all claim as mentioned that unfit, unmerciful (dead spiritually) sinners are saved by grace and thereby obtain mercy. Whilst Jesus said it is the merciful who obtain mercy. GT says it is from among those who are unrighteous and have no desire for it that God redeems. Whilst Jesus says it is those who hunger and thirst for righteousness who are filled. Both cannot be untrue and I believe Jesus is true!

These things which as shown are in contradiction to Jesus' teaching are also contrary to God's character. God in GT is said to stop an evil man in his tracks 'in His grace' by a 'Damascus Road like' experience. This is contrary to the character and whole nature of God. The Spirit of God is shown us with clear fruit:

> . . . love, joy, peace, longsuffering, kindness, goodness, faithfulness, *gentleness, self-control*.
> *Galatians 5:22-23 italics mine*

And self-control involves not imposing what one wishes upon another. This is God's Nature.

Paul's conversion was not against his heart's true desire as I explained in chapter 12 entitled *The apostles Paul and Judas*. GT says it was contrary to Paul's evil heart that God did this: Another lie.

Neither was God's hardening of Pharaoh's heart against Pharaoh's own intentions in the time of Moses and the Exodus. In chapter 10 *Understanding Romans 9*, I explain how 6 times Pharaoh hardened his heart before the Lord stepped in and strengthened Pharaoh in that resolve (to continue; not 'change') a further 6 times.

God responds to ability witnessed in the heart of the individual, whilst GT says there is nothing good in man. I explain how the belief that man is

100% disabled is false in chapter 21 entitled *Journey into Light*.

There is another thing GT is opposed to in Romans 9: it is opposed to God's mercy being for the merciful – as Jesus quoted above clearly says – when God says '***I will have mercy on whomever I will have mercy***' (Romans 9:15) GT instead suggests this is for anyone whom God wants, irrespective of whether the individual themselves desire to be merciful or not. GT makes clear that this saying by God involves the salvation of whomever God chooses without precondition, and indeed this '**mercy**' – this 'Grace' [hence the name 'Grace Theology'] – is invariably upon those who are unmerciful and unfit sinners: Whilst the very nature of God causes release of His Spirit only in the lives of those hungry for righteousness. Jesus clearly said it is those who are merciful who go on to obtain mercy. How this works with predestination I explain according to Paul's own thinking in Romans 8 within chapter 11 – *Romans 8:28 in Context*. Always a 'conditional' situation in Paul's teaching.

GT claims instead that God is being capricious in saying,

> . . . *I will have mercy on whomever I will have mercy.* Romans 9:15

It explains this as God picking out whom He wills to be merciful to, wholly irrespective of the recipient's request or desire for it. This is a lie. It is heresy. The very context where this quote belongs – as explained in chapter 10 – demonstrates that it is those who have not sinned in unbelief who receive mercy.

The bible does not contradict itself. Jesus made plain who gets mercy and who will benefit from being filled with righteousness. Indeed Jesus is not alone in saying it (as if His words were not enough!):

> With the merciful You will show Yourself merciful . . .
> *2 Samuel 22:26*

Is it any wonder God hates Grace Theology?

NINETEEN

THE PREDESTINATION CHALLENGE

——

For a number of years the following has been a challenge posted on the Jarom web site:

> IF YOU HAVE BEEN BROUGHT UP TO BELIEVE
> IN 'UNCONDITIONAL ELECTION', THE IDEA THAT
> GOD HAS ALREADY PICKED ALL THOSE WHO WILL
> BE SAVED, THEN THIS IS FOR YOU.
>
> THE QUESTION IS: WHAT VERSE OR PASSAGE OF THE
> BIBLE HELPS YOU TO BELIEVE THAT THIS IS SO?
>
> MY CHALLENGE IS TO BE GIVEN A VERSE OR PASSAGE
> WHICH CANNOT BE SEEN OR EXPLAINED ANOTHER
> WAY.

Then on the 8th January 2003 I added a further challenge:

> THE IDOL CHALLENGE TO PREDESTINATION
> THINKERS: A CHALLENGE TO SEE IF JESUS IS LORD
> AND 1ST OR THE DOCTRINES OF 'CALVINISM',

209

'REFORMED THINKING', 'UNCONDITIONAL PRE-
DESTINATION' (THE WHOLE DEAL OF 'GRACE
THEOLOGY'). IF JESUS AND HIS KINGDOM IS 1ST
IN YOUR LIFE, THEN THE FRUITS EXPLAINED IN
THE LINKED ARTICLE WILL NOT BE IN YOUR LIFE.
IF THESE FRUITS ARE THERE, THEN YOU HAVE
A 'HOLY COW' IN THIS 'DOCTRINE' AND NEED
TO REPENT OF YOUR IDOLATRY. THE ARTICLE IS
ENTITLED *MAKING AN IDOL?*

For the sake of completeness I have converted the article
just mentioned and it appears now as the next chapter.

When this challenge was a set of pages on the
internet you would have seen more bible passages
then are here. I refer the reader therefore to the list
of bible passages at the back of the book. All the
significant passages explained fully elsewhere have not
been repeated here and are no longer under this named
challenge but elsewhere in the book.

First about T.U.L.I.P

Ever heard of the acronym T.U.L.I.P ?

This is said to be the 5 points of Calvinism.

Total Depravity or, **T**otal Inability
Unconditional election (predestination)
Limited atonement
Irresistible Grace
Preservation of the saints

Well, let's deal with each of these themes in turn.
Not spending any more time than is necessary to just
briefly repudiate each one:

THE PREDESTINATION CHALLENGE

T OF T.U.L.I.P

This stands for Total Depravity or, Total Inability.

Total depravity: the idea that Fallen Man is so depraved – in himself – that he is unable to turn to God without God touching him first and without God enabling him first to turn to Him.

Such a belief makes utter nonsense of Ezekiel 18:32 ' **"For I have no pleasure in the death of one who dies," says the Lord GOD. "Therefore turn and live!"** '

Tell me honestly, if a man is unable to turn, would God make such a statement?

See also the chapter *Journey into Light* for other passages of the Bible to show no man is totally dead spiritually.

U OF T.U.L.I.P

U stands for: **Unconditional election** (predestination): the idea that God has already picked all those who will be saved and therefore all those who will not.

This makes nonsense of the Word of God which clearly states in 2 Peter 3:9: '**The Lord is . . . not willing that any should perish but that all should come to repentance**'. Equally it is against 1 Timothy 2:4 where God is seen as one who '**desires all men to be saved . . .**' In case you were in any doubt both the Greek verbs *boulomai* and *thelò* are used which means that both God's desire, 'His wish', and 'His purpose' are involved. There is no plan by God to prevent anyone from being saved. Equally there is no plan to save some above others because as mentioned several times as with Deuteronomy 10:17 '**. . . the LORD . . . shows no partiality . . .**'

L OF T.U.L.I.P

L stands for **Limited atonement**: the idea that the death of Jesus and his shed blood only paid for those who end up saved.

You do not have to go far to see how non biblical such a belief is. In 1 John 2:1-2 we read '**. . . we have an Advocate with the Father, Jesus Christ the righteous. And He Himself is the propitiation for our sins, and not for ours only but also for the whole world.**'

The propitiation means the substitute sacrifice. Jesus' death on the cross was not just for the sake of the saints, those reading the letter '**our**' above, but also for everybody else '**the whole world**'. The context is clear '**our**' and '**ours**' refers to Jew and Gentile believers since both are within those who '**have fellowship with us . . . with the Father and with His Son Jesus Christ**' (1 John 1:3). Everyone else is then covered by '**the whole world**'.

Equally when Jesus' substitution sacrifice is prophesied in Isaiah the '**All**' that sin is the '**all**' that is covered/paid for: '**All we like sheep have gone astray; we have turned, every one, to his own way; and the LORD has laid on Him the iniquity of us all**' (Isaiah 53:6): everyone.

Jesus is explicit that the Father, '**Makes His sun rise on the evil and on the good, and sends rain on the just and on the unjust**' (Matthew 5:45) So that, *Just because a table is covered in food and provision sufficient for all, it does not mean all benefit. Only those who partake: That is the witness of scripture in regards to salvation.*

I OF T.U.L.I.P

I stands for **Irresistible Grace**: the idea that God's enabling of fallen man by a gift of initial faith cannot be refused by man: he has no choice in the matter: it cannot be resisted.

This makes nonsense of Jesus' words in Matthew 23:37 '. . . **I wanted to gather your children together, as a hen gathers her chicks under *her* wings, but you were not willing!**'

God was willing, but these people were not. They resisted what God wanted: Which is why we as believers are also told in 1 Thessalonians 5:19 not to '**quench the Spirit**'. God's nature involves '**self-control**' (Galatians 5:23) such that He is '**willing to yield**' (James 3:17) so that any persistent refusal to accept what God gives effectively resists His Grace.

The issue of God's sovereignty versus free-will is sometimes a red herring when really God's sovereignty is versus His Self-control.

P OF T.U.L.I.P

P stands for **Preservation of the saints**: the idea that

it is impossible for a true 'elect' person to return to a state where loss of faith occurs such that they end up lost.

'Once saved always saved' would be another way of putting it.

Whilst it is true that Jesus said '**My Father . . . is greater than all; and no one is able to snatch *them* out of My Father's hand**' (John 10:29) there is therefore complete security for all those desiring to stay in the Father's hand. The Word is also clear that you can, if involved in a clearly persisting walk, step out of His hand. Jesus' statement relates to security from outside, not to retaining those who do not want to stay. 'God will not force into heaven someone who does not want to be there!' Which is why Paul wrote to believers, fellow saints, in Romans 11:22: '**Therefore consider the goodness and severity of God: on those who fell, severity; but toward you, goodness, if you continue in *His* goodness. Otherwise you also will be cut off.**'

It is explicit that it is possible to '**be cut off**' if there is a clear discontinuance in goodness. It is either impossible or possible for a true believer to eventually be cut off: which one does the bible say?

Beyond T.U.L.I.P
Having looked at T.U.L.I.P let's look at passages often used to back up unconditional predestination.

Bible passages

To start off, let's deal with passages with the word 'elect' or 'chosen' translated from the Greek *eklektos*

> . . . many are called, but few chosen. *Matthew 20:16*

> . . . many are called, but few *are* chosen.
> *Matthew 22:14*

> . . . for the elect's sake those days will be shortened.
> *Matthew 24:22*

> . . . so as to deceive, if possible, even the elect.
> *Matthew 24:24*

> . . . they will gather together His elect from . . .
> *Matthew 24:31*

> . . . for the elect's sake, whom He chose, He shortened the days . . .   *Mark 13:20*

In **Mark 13:20** the words '**whom He chose**', could give the idea that the 'special' are chosen i.e. to salvation, but the text is about the good guys that remain at the end and there is no inference to salvation. It is the righteous who have been picked to go through the tribulation which are in view.

> . . . to deceive, if possible, even the elect. *Mark 13:22*

> . . . gather together His elect from the four winds . . .
> *Mark 13:27*

> . . . shall God not avenge His own elect who . . .
> *Luke 18:7*

Who shall bring a charge against God's elect?
Romans 8:33

... as *the* elect of God, holy and beloved, put on ...
Colossians 3:12

... I endure all things for the sake of the elect ...
2 Timothy 2:10

... according to the faith of God's elect ... *Titus 1:1*

... elect according to the foreknowledge of God the Father ... *1 Peter 1:2*

... rejected indeed by men, but chosen by God *and* precious ... *1 Peter 2:4*

In **1 Peter 2:4** the verb 'to choose' is not present in the Greek, but the adjective *eklektos* in the Accusative case, so the phrase '**by God**' should precede the adjectives in contrast to the preceding words '**rejected indeed by men**'. This therefore reads like this as a contrast '**but with God choice, precious**' as translated by *Young's Literal Translation of the Holy Bible*.

... you *are* a chosen generation, a royal priesthood
... 1 Peter 2:9

... those *who are* with Him *are* called, chosen, and faithful. *Revelation 17:14*

All these passages are discussed by means of a thorough look at the way the word *eklektos* was understood when the New Testament was written. In chapter 16 I gave a good number of examples from that research to show that *eklektos* is well translated with an emphasis on 'quality' so the above – in the light of the way *eklektos* is commonly used in the Septuagint – is well read as 'precious', 'righteous', 'good guys', etc. It is quality that is the emphasis. So that when Jesus said '**many are called, but few *eklektos***' he is saying few are fit for the calling, few are up to it.

Other passages

Exodus 4:11

> So the LORD said to him, 'Who has made man's mouth? Or who makes the mute, the deaf, the seeing, or the blind? *Have* not I, the LORD?'

This verse is used to defend the concept that predestination is valid in all things.

The verse is part of a defence by God of His call on Moses to lead Israel out of Egypt. Moses' had argued in verse 10 '**. . . but I *am* slow of speech and slow of tongue.**' In other words the Lord was saying I knew you were this way, but I want to use you as you are. Don't let that bother you or be a hindrance to you. '**Now therefore, go, and I will be with your mouth and teach you what you shall say.**' (Exodus 4:12).

Just as we could add whether you are a boy or, a girl is not your choice; born free or, a slave, in rich

217

circumstances or, in a desert landscape, etcetera, I do not see a reference or inference to salvation whatsoever.

Proverbs 16:1

> The preparations of the heart *belong* to man, but the answer of the tongue *is* from the LORD.

This verse is used in the understanding that the Lord's influence is such that what comes out of the tongue is His doing irrespective of what is in the heart. This perception of the verse gives the idea that unconditional predestination is unavoidable in all things. A man is helpless in what he says.

This understanding is directly against Jesus' words '**. . . out of the abundance of the heart the mouth speaks. A good man out of the good treasure of his heart brings forth good things, and an evil man out of the evil treasure brings forth evil things.**' (Matthew 12:34-35). It is not therefore irrespective of what is in the heart that the tongue speaks; it is directly linked to what is in the heart.

What I believe Proverbs 16:1 is about: Robert Young's literal translation gives '**Of man *are* arrangements of the heart, and from Jehovah an answer of the tongue.**' In other words the Lord's involvement is not here in what comes out of the tongue, but it is in the response to what the tongue says. Just as James tells us that '**each one is tempted when he is drawn away by his own desires and enticed. Then, when**

desire has conceived, it gives birth to sin . . .' (James 1:14-15). What you think, what is in your heart is not sin full grown until it produces a fruit. The fruit mentioned in Proverbs is what the tongue brings forth. It is to that fruit which the Lord answers.

Of course we must not forget that Jesus said if you lust after a woman it is a sin, but His emphasis is not on a passing temptation in your mind. It is a wilful and active lusting response to that temptation (Matthew 5:28). Let not the enemy condemn you when you recognise the temptation in your mind, confess it to the Lord and state the opposite desire. You have not sinned. If you however dwell on it, pursue it, or, activate it deliberately, then you are guilty.

Having responded further by a 'confession' of what is in the heart (not unlike Romans 10:10), then the Lord steps in judgment accordingly (Hence conversely, the importance of confession: owning up to the Lord). Therefore Proverbs 16:1 speaks about the reply (from the Lord) as the reaping of the spoken evil or good out of the abundance of the heart: That is to say, **'the answer of the tongue.'** In other words God ensures you reap what you sow (Galatians 6:7-8). In this appreciation Proverbs 16:1 is not a reference to predestination.

Proverbs 16:4

The LORD has made all *things* for Himself, yes, even the wicked for the day of doom.

This verse is understandably easy to see as useable to say God creates even the wicked and therefore man has no say in the matter. Man is unable to change from the fate given him is the teaching of unconditional predestination.

Due to the Hebrew word *paal* from which 'made' has been translated the translation in the NIV is closer the mark **'The LORD works out everything for his own ends- even the wicked for a day of disaster.'** This is more regularly translated as the verb 'work' (19), or 'do' (10) then it is, 'make' (4) in the KJV: Thus readily visible as an action upon something existing rather than the cause (the creation) of the existence.

They have to become wicked first. His use of them does not mean He set them up to be or desired them to be. That would be against His nature since **'God is light and in Him is no darkness at all'** (1 John 1:5). The emphasis is on God making use of the wicked for His own purposes: Which is what happened to Pharaoh in Egypt when Moses came to lead the people of Israel out of Egypt (see chapter 10 *Understanding Romans 9*).

Proverbs 16:9

> A man's heart plans his way, but the LORD directs
> his steps.

This verse is said to mean that whatever a man decides, the Lord causes his steps to be what He purposes. Irrespective of the plan made in the heart what happens is out of the hands of man. Man's salvation is not determined by his heart's plans. Unconditional predestination assumes the Lord does not allow man to choose and by this verse it would say that no desire for righteousness in man would make the Lord to bring it about.

This verse is part of the general themes and thinking in Proverbs 16. See Proverbs 16:1 and Proverbs 16:4. In other words it is saying that what a man plans have limits as to their effectiveness. They are fruitful in their true origin in that '. . . **whatever a man sows, that he will also reap.**' (Galatians 6:7). That is to say whether out of a heart desiring righteousness or not. But, this does not mean the outcome is always what was desired or planned for. If in your greed you plan to make money oblivious of others, then you may find your plans ineffective or, short term (James 4:13-16; Luke 12:16-20). If you plan to harm others you may do so, but limits will be 'brought into play'. Same as for desiring good and planning for it, you will often be led in a path of learning and refining before this plan fully comes to pass. Joseph is a good example (Genesis 37-50; John 15:2b). So my reply to this verse's use for unconditional predestination is similar to that of Proverbs 16:1 and Proverbs 16:4. God uses and changes the boundaries around people's lives to fit His purposes and to reward according to the fruit of their doings (Jeremiah 17:9-10).

This is not to say salvation is chosen for one and not another. There is no inference or reference to it in this text. Indeed Jesus said emphatically '**Blessed** *are* **those who hunger and thirst for righteousness, for they shall be filled.**' (Matthew 5:6). This is in direct contrast to the understanding given for unconditional election's perception of Proverbs 16:9.

1 Corinthians 1:18-31

> For the message of the cross is foolishness to those who are perishing, but to us who are being saved it is the power of God. For it is written: '*I will destroy the wisdom of the wise, and bring to nothing the understanding of the prudent.*' . . . For you see your calling, brethren, that not many wise according to the flesh, not many mighty, not many noble, *are called.* But God has chosen the foolish things of the world to put to shame the wise, and God has chosen the weak things of the world to put to shame the things which are mighty . . . that no flesh should glory in His presence . . . that, as it is written, '*He who glories, let him glory in the LORD.*'

In Paul saying it '**is foolishness to those who are perishing**', it is said that because they are perishing they are unable to make sense of it. No one can understand the message of the cross if they are pre-ordained to perish. This passage is also used to say that all the glory for salvation goes to the Lord since He did the choosing. Thus this is said to support the teaching of unconditional predestination.

However, Paul is not saying that there are none which are wise or none which are influential that are saved, just few. But who are those perishing? It is none other than those who do not believe. But, this passage does not inform us as to how they believe nor at what stage, etc. Romans 8 does that and I recommend chapter 11 *Romans 8:28 in context* which explains this. It is those who in their hearts have refused the revelation given to them who are blinded and to whom the message is foolish. Since '**as many as received Him, to them He gave the right to become children of God**' The gift of the right to become a child of God is bestowed after Jesus' revelation has been received. Not due to some choice before their lifetime by God, but Scripture says by the individual in their lifetime (John 1:12).

Revelation 13:8

> And all who dwell on the earth will worship him, whose names have not been written in the Book of Life of the Lamb slain from the foundation of the world.

If people's names are written in a book from the foundation of the world as to the fact that they will be partakers of eternal life then unconditional pre-destination is a reality.

However, I read this as that *the Lamb was slain from the foundation of the world*: The plan of salvation having been prepared from the beginning. Not that the names on the Book of Life have been written on there from the beginning. But this would appear not supported by Revelation 17:8 since the Lamb is not mentioned. I have taken that to mean that the Lord has from the beginning had the Book of Life, but as the wicked practise their unbelief they are blotted out of the book.

Because, if Jesus' words are to be taken seriously about a name being blotted out, then it is impossible that all were known from the beginning. You can't have names blotted out if you know all who will eventually make it from the start. Since then they would not be written in.

> He who overcomes shall be clothed in white garments, and I will not blot out his name from the Book of Life; but I will confess his name before My Father and before His angels. *Revelation 3:5*

If the possibility is not there for a name to be blotted out, then the inference is that Jesus is being devious. A blasphemy upon the God Who:

> . . . is light and in Him is no darkness at all.
> *1 John 1:5*

Revelation 17:8

> The beast that you saw was, and is not, and will ascend out of the bottomless pit and go to perdition.

And those who dwell on the earth will marvel, whose names are not written in the Book of Life from the foundation of the world, when they see the beast that was, and is not, and yet is.

The answer to this is the same as for Revelation 13:8, it is the Book of Life that has been from the foundation of the world. This is testified from the fact that names can be blotted out of the Book. There is indeed no inference upon a written up and unchanged contents of a book from the beginning, but instead it is the wicked which shun the Light that gives light to every man who comes into the world (John 1:9; John 3:20). The evil heart that rejects the Light is the heart that will marvel at the Beast.

Passages not covered in this chapter are either found elsewhere in the book or covered by the type of reply appropriate to the particular thought contained in that passage: e.g. if the group is in view, then the meaning is like in Ephesians 1 as expounded in chapter 13.

Now let's look at the idol challenge. Reading the next chapter will help you identify if you have an idol in your life.

TWENTY

MAKING AN IDOL?

———

What is an idol?

An idol is anything which is put in the place of God in your life. Particularly it is anything which you worship or spend much time thinking about. Inevitably it is something or someone which you would gladly talk about almost anytime.

The purpose of this chapter is to identify what an idol is and how to check if you have one. If you then find yourself as with an idol and you do not wish this, you can then begin to address that with help of a prayer at the end.

An idol can be an object, a person, a teaching or ideal or, anything which takes up the place of God. It is particularly relevant to believers as it is that which is placed before the God whom they know. For the Christian it is that which is put before God and His kingdom – His purposes. Jesus said:

> If anyone comes to Me and does not hate his father
> and mother, wife and children, brothers and sisters,
> yes, and his own life also, he cannot be My disciple.
>
> *Luke 14:26*

The moment you become a Christian you are in a warfare footing. You are in God's army and you have an enemy: the Devil and his minions. He knows that you become less effective for the Kingdom of God if you place anything as of greater value than God or, His purposes. And that is what happens on a regular basis if you have an idol.

This is so fundamental to the warfare believers are involved in that Satan has made available demons to deceive believers specifically in the area of idols. These will deceive believers to believe and to go on believing something is more important than God at any level. We know demons are directly involved where idols are concerned because Paul stated:

> What am I saying then? That an idol is anything, or
> what is offered to idols is anything? But *I* say that
> the things which the Gentiles sacrifice they sacrifice
> to demons and not to God, and I do not want you to
> have fellowship with demons.
>
> *1 Corinthians 10:19-20*

What are the effects of having an idol?

The attention and love you have for God and the attention and love you have for people is directly affected by an idol.

Because the idol is felt important it causes all contact with others who have stated otherwise to be shunned or, looked down upon. They are the ones 'missing out'. Knowing this idol is more important than knowing those who do not think so. The way others are treated is a good indicator of having an idol.

Another good indicator of an idol is how captivated you are with Jesus, your Lord in worship. When in fellowship with other believers, during worship an idol will come to mind regularly. If, as mentioned above you are with others who do not see the importance you have for your idol, then in worship times another sign is to be conscious of those people and think of them as needing help – incomplete or, even harmful.

Why should these effects occur?

As the scripture above shows demons have a direct interest in idols. This being so they feed the mind with accusations about others. They remind the idol worshipper of the idol to take the place of the Lord in a worship time. They will direct the individual to the idol when insecurities are present.

As with any deception the classic fruits apply: domination (control), isolation, exclusivity, accusing of the brethren. With an idol this is in direct link to that idol. If the idol is a teaching or, an idea then as Jesus stated:

. . . wisdom is justified by all her children. *Luke 7:35*

In other words, the teaching even though it may be good in itself (see note below) is held in higher esteem than the Lord or, the Kingdom. The teaching is not held as a tool for a job, but as the tool, the master, the answer. The believer acts as child of the teaching. You don't hold it; it holds you.

The outworking of this is that if you are in leadership then anything the Lord wishes to do with someone else can be quenched or redirected in accord with the idol. Progress is made if the idol is given it's proper due. If someone has a call from the Lord to do something and there are steps towards that which are known, the idol is often imposed as needing to be addressed before this calling or these steps are freely permitted.

The teaching will be carried out regularly lest a lack of faithfulness to the idol is perceived. Shelves of this idea or teaching will be full of books prominently displayed. Preaching involves mentioning this idol regularly – often without fail – right down to including it or, making it the prominent theme in say, a wedding speech or sermon. Is this putting the couple first and that occasion?

Demons not only accuse the 'unbeliever' in the mind of the idol worshipper, but they will where access is given, place or, impose whatever feelings they can on the 'unbeliever' to make them bow to the 'believer': Or, to seek help from the 'believer' – the idol worshipper. The standing of the 'unbeliever' in the minds of the 'believer' is affected by the 'taking on board' of the feelings as their own. These kinds of feelings can outwardly look very real and honest. But the 'unbeliever' is actually not reacting out of himself or herself, but out of what is spiritually imposed. If the 'unbeliever' truly submits to these then they become a 'believer' in the minds of the idol worshipper and are 'accepted'. Lasting peace and security do not come from this however and further 'bowing down' is felt as the way forward whilst in fact the opposite is true. Jesus alone is the source of peace.

A prayer
I have borrowed much of the prayer at the end of the online article entitled *The Characteristics of Deception* (www.jarom.net)

If in reading you are already conscious of an idol then be honest with God and share this with Him. Turn from following this idol and instead hold it in its proper place. It may be valuable and important, but never as important as The Lord and His purposes. Ask for His help in this.

Dear Father,

Thank you that you are Light and in you is no darkness at all.

I ask that you shine your light in me and reveal all the beliefs and thoughts

which I have taken on board as if from you, but in reality are not of you.

I want to believe what is from you and nothing from the enemy.

Just as you asked the church at Laodicea to anoint their eyes with eye salve

that they may see, so I ask that you anoint my eyes that I may see.

I ask this as I may be blind to idols in my life and ask that you reveal them.

Show me where my worship to you is interfered by an idol.

Show me where my relationship with others are influenced by an idol.

I repent and reject all idols (name any here).

It is only you that I want as first in my life.

And it is you alone I wish to have as Lord.

Thank you that you promise to forgive all those who confess their sins to you.

I receive your forgiveness now.

Thank you.

I thank you that the Holy Spirit will guide into all truth.

I ask for discernment and courage to unlearn wrong things received

as well as prevent new things which attempt to make a home in me.

Help me to recognise any fresh work of the enemy

which attempts to divert me from your ways.

Thank you that you give wisdom freely to those who
ask.

Father I ask all this in Jesus' Name,
Amen

(1 John 1:5; Revelation 3:18;
John 16:13; James 1:5-8; John 16:23)

NOTE

This chapter first arose as an article written in general terms
within the understanding of how the enemy works. No teaching
is mentioned or alluded to within this chapter. However in saying
a teaching may be good, the observant reader will note that this
book makes explicit claim that unconditional predestination to
salvation for individuals is not biblical. Therefore it is not regarded
as a 'good' teaching.

TWENTY ONE

JOURNEY INTO LIGHT

—

In this chapter you will read from the bible that no man is wholly dead. A total spiritual death sometimes spoken of as 'total depravity' or 'total inability' is not biblical. What the bible shows instead is that from his natural birth onwards there is a journey into Light.

The Bible tells us,

> . . . God is light and in Him is no darkness at all.
>
> *1 John 1:5*

Since He is also known as,

> . . . the Alpha and the Omega, the Beginning and the End. *Revelation 21:6*

It then follows that any journey into Light starts and ends with God. The journey started at our creation.

> In the beginning . . . God said, 'Let Us make man in
> Our image, according to Our likeness . . .' So God
> created man in His *own* image; in the image of God
> He created him; male and female He created them . . .
> the LORD God formed man *of* the dust of the ground,
> and breathed life into his nostrils the breath of life;
> and man became a living being.
>
> *Genesis 1:1, 26-27, 2:7*

Now, this is not recorded for any other of God's
creatures. So, on two counts we are different from all
others. First we are created in God's image and second,
He has breathed life into us. God is not on record as
breathing of Himself into any other creature. And, there
is no other understood as being made in His image.
Whatever we may think of our fellow man there is no
other creature like him in this respect.

The journey then begins with a relationship with
God which involves His instruction.

> Then God blessed them, and God said to them, 'Be
> fruitful and multiply; fill the earth and subdue it;
> have dominion over the fish of the sea, over the birds
> of the air, and over every living thing that moves on
> the earth.'
>
> *Genesis 1:28*

God also tells our first parents that the food available
to them involves the vegetation that has been created.
And that it is the same for all the animals. This was
to change after the Flood, but that is how it began.
He then places Adam, before Eve came along, into a

garden as a first dwelling place – A home to begin life on earth and to look after. In this garden He also placed two trees – The tree of life and the tree of knowledge of good and evil. Of this second tree the Lord said:

> . . . Of every tree of the garden you may freely eat; but of the tree of the knowledge of good and evil you shall not eat, for in the day that you eat of it you shall surely die. *Genesis 2:16-17*

The Literal Hebrew, the language the Old Testament of the Bible is written in is like this:

> . . . in the day that you eat of it dying you shall die. *Genesis 2:17 with margin note included*

The Lord begins also to spend time with Adam and in this time He brings before Adam animals and He enjoys seeing what Adam calls them. On another occasion, as the Lord desired to spend time with Adam, we read:

> . . . they heard the sound of the LORD God walking in the garden in the cool of the day, and Adam and his wife hid themselves from the presence of the LORD God among the trees of the garden. Then the LORD God called to Adam and said to him, 'Where *are* you?' *Genesis 3:8-9*

Eve was with Adam now and they hid themselves because they had eaten of the forbidden fruit. This had caused them to realise they were naked and in this recognition they decided to hide. The journey away from God had begun.

Were they now dead?

No. We saw that God said a process of dying would take effect:

> . . . in the day that you eat of it dying you shall die.
> *Genesis 2:17*

So they did not die completely, but part of them began to die. They did not die on that day physically nor, did they die wholly spiritually. We not only know that they did not die physically and that this was because others had their blood shed in their place. But, we also know that spiritually the life within was not extinguished.

In the recognition that Adam and Eve now needed clothing we read,

> . . . for Adam and his wife the LORD God made tunics of skin, and clothed them. *Genesis 3:21*

(Who said the Lord had no interest in fashion?)

His use of animal skins, leather, meant that He is on record as the first person to shed blood. This blood shed meant the life of those animals was shed in place of the life-blood of Adam and Eve. So we see that there was a way to spare them from death. By temporary substitution – a permanent one was to follow.

But, were they now spiritually lifeless?

Were they unable to respond to God without some fresh input on His part? Certainly dimmed spiritual insight and deception had begun to take effect in their lives from the moment the Devil's lies took hold – Thus veiling their eyes to the light for their way. But, God is seen as aware and expectant, of a spiritual ability within man throughout scripture: An ability that could allow for more light to be accessed.

How can this be?
We saw that in the beginning at Creation God not only made man in His own image, but He breathed life into him. This did not occur with any other being. Of all the creatures God has made we are the only ones recorded as God having breathed life into (Genesis 2:7). God implanted a piece of Himself in us. Can God die? No.

But, this life in us is dependent on us to enable its growth or, our eventual separation from 'it'. Our receipt and acceptance of Him as described in John 1:12 enables God's subsequent (gift) right to become children of God.

Our rejection of Him eventually causes what we 'have' to be taken away. Jesus speaks about what we 'have' in this way:

> For whoever has, to him more will be given, and he will have abundance; but whoever does not have, even what he has will be taken away from him.
>
> *Matthew 13:12; Matthew 25:29;*
> *Mark 4:25; Luke 8:18; Luke 19:26*

If you have a desire for righteousness, then more will be given you. If you do not, then your ability to desire for righteousness itself will be taken from you. God will test you to see what is in your heart and what you sow out of that heart you shall reap (Galatians 6:7-8; Revelation 2:23 et al.).

Scripture is clear that everyone 'has' even though they are not born again. No one is totally dead that they have nothing with which to respond to the Light who is in the world. To respond to Jesus as,

> . . . the true Light which gives light to every man
> who comes into the world.   *John 1:9*

How Do We Know This?

One pointer as shown is Jesus saying 'whoever does not have, even what he has will be taken away from him'. Everyone 'has' something which can eventually be taken away.

Animals do not share this 'life'. They have not been 'breathed' into by God. Now in Hebrew 'breath' is synonymous with 'spirit'. And since God is a Spirit, this is what is in us all to the measure that scripture indicates. Unlike animals, when we die, this 'spirit' returns to God. Thus showing itself to have remained untainted by 'the fall' or, sin. Regarding this difference this is the record:

> All go to one place: all are from the dust, and all
> return to dust. Who knows the spirit of the sons of

240

men, which goes upward, and the spirit of the beast,
which goes down to the earth?   *Ecclesiastes 3:20-21*

Then the dust will return to the earth as it was, and
the spirit will return to God who gave it.
Ecclesiastes 12:7

We know this is talking about God's spirit 'part' within
us because the scripture also shows this:

If He should set His heart on it, *if* He should gather
to Himself His Spirit and His breath, all flesh would
perish together, and man would return to dust.
Job 34:14-15

This is why God is known as Father of all, because
He is:

. . . the God of the spirits of all flesh . . .
Numbers 16:22

. . . the LORD, the God of the spirits of all flesh . . .
Numbers 27:16

The idea that the disobedience of Adam caused the
complete tainting of all of his being and his posterity
is false. The part or aspect of man's being which is
untainted is that which enables receipt and response
to God's revelation to all: The area of our being which
is conceived with us at the inception of our existence.
This is what we all 'have' as Jesus put it when he said

'even what he "has" shall be taken away' as quoted above.

When God gave the instruction not to eat of the fruit He did not say you shall die and that this death was going to render ineffective spiritual activity or awareness without new and fresh input by God. As we saw the literal Hebrew of what God said to Adam is '**in the day that you eat of it *dying you shall die***' (Genesis 2:17 – my emphasis) as explained in many Bible margins. Adam did not die on that day, but a process of dying began. A process that did not 'touch' or affect the life God placed within which can not die. But – we – can separate ourselves from it. And this then causes what Jesus said '**even what he has will be taken away from him**'.

We know that Adam still had a means to do what was right. We know this because when God spoke to Adam's first son Cain, God told him that if he did what was right he would be accepted? And, that this would prevent sin from having its way. The express result being that Cain would be acceptable to God.

If this ability is in Cain, it is in Adam and his posterity: all of us.

> So the LORD said to Cain . . . If you do well, will you not be accepted? And if you do not do well, sin lies at the door. And its desire *is* for you, but you should rule over it. *Genesis 4:6-7*

There is a call of God and expectation of this ability throughout scripture even amongst the most wicked.

> . . . if a wicked man turns from all his sins which
> he has committed, keeps all My statutes, and does
> what is lawful and right, he shall surely live; he shall
> not die. None of the transgressions which he has
> committed shall be remembered against him; because
> of the righteousness which he has done, he shall live.
> 'Do I have any pleasure at all that the wicked should
> die?' says the Lord GOD, '*and* not that he should
> turn from his ways and live?' *Ezekiel 18:21-23*

Even in a passage popular as a 'proof text' to say
otherwise there is clear inherent ability alluded to. I am
referring to Ephesians 2:1 which in English reads '**you
He made alive, who were dead in trespasses and
sins**'. This is read as saying that God made alive dead
people: Folk with no life to respond to God with. As I
have explained before and think safe to repeat, the 'in'
here is only valid from the Greek original if understood
'whilst in'. The New Testament section of the Bible
was first written in Greek. The Greek for 'in' is *en*, but
it is not found in Verse One. It can be found in Verse
Two, but not this one. The reason it is used in English
is that the words '**the trespasses and the sins**' are in
a grammatical form known as the Dative. The use of
the Dative here is to indicate *the means by which* they
were '**dead**'. This is known as the instrumental use of
the Dative. So that, it is *whilst active in* trespasses and
sins that they 'were dead': Clearly implying an ability
to not be active in sin. Ephesians 2:1 therefore is an
indicator of ability to turn from sin.

Yes, the Bible tells us we are all sinners for '**all have sinned**' (Romans 3:23), but as shown above it also says we are able to turn from sin. It is also mentioned that '**in Adam all die**' (1 Corinthians 15:22) but, by the measure of the Spirit within each of us we can look to Christ to have Life.

This chapter contains much of the chapter by the same title taken out of the book *Will there be Non-Christians in heaven? – with The Meaning of Born Again*

Let us now conclude.

TWENTY TWO

IN CONCLUSION

—

So, do you think you're chosen?

Well, Ephesians says this,

> Blessed *be* the God and Father of our Lord Jesus Christ,
> who has blessed us with every spiritual blessing in
> the heavenly *places* in Christ, just as He chose us
> in Him before the foundation of the world, that we
> should be holy and without blame before Him in
> love, having predestined us to adoption as sons by
> Jesus Christ to Himself . . . *Ephesians 1:3-5*

If you are in Christ – in Him – then, yes you are
chosen. As part of the body of Christ we are chosen.

No individual is mentioned in the bible except
for Jesus as predestined before the foundation of the
world. He is the Lamb slain from the foundation of
the world (1 Peter 1:20; Revelation 13:8).

God desires all men to be saved, is not willing that any should perish and has no pleasure in the death of the wicked. No individual has been picked to be lost in eternity (1 Timothy 2:4; 2 Peter 3:9; Ezekiel 18:23).

Instead everyone is found alive because God's breath – a piece of Himself – is in each of them. This enables a response to Jesus who by His Spirit is the Light that gives light to every man who comes into the world. Everyone who then receives Him – takes hold of that Revelation for themselves – is then given the right to become a child of God. This is the explicit cause and effect written in scripture (Ecclesiastes 12:7; John 1:9; John 1:12).

This is when God's conditional predestination kicks in. Seeing the heart of the person loving God, though sometimes not knowing this is so, God sets the person up to a call. The practise of righteousness is testimony to this heart (Romans 8:27-30 in context; John 3:21; Romans 2:7).

> If you know that He is righteous, you know that everyone who practises righteousness is born of Him.
> *1 John 2:29*

There are two groups in the bible: the righteous and the wicked. You choose which group you are in. How? (Ezekiel 18:19-32)

By receiving Christ you are in the righteous group.

The reason there is a party in heaven every time a sinner repents is because it is down to each of us to do so. The rejoicing is real in recognition that this repentance is what God wants and delights in. It is a testimony to His self-control over His sovereignty. God wants with Him only those who want Him in eternity. It is their choice and His joy (Luke 15:7).

So, what is the simple truth of the bible in regards to unconditional predestination?

Since '**God is light and in Him is no darkness at all**', then it follows that there is no evil or sin in God. Since God desires no sin to occur, then He desires no one to sin. Now, if none sinned as He desires, then none would be lost as He desires. If none were lost as God desires, then none are picked to be saved since He desires all to be saved. (1 John 1:5)

That is the testimony of the bible to the true God of love and grace.

Now, let's give the world hope. Let's tell them about Jesus.

An Epilogue

A MESSAGE TO BIBLE SOCIETIES

Translation is a challenging task, especially when it involves languages no longer in daily use. So the work of translation is important. Not least is the fact that everyone who does not use this original language today is often totally reliant on the honesty and sincerity of the translator. I therefore applaud all who carry that work in spirit and in truth.

The translation of the bible is dependent on the understanding of the text being translated. This can never be done out of a vacuum of doctrine and belief. It is unavoidable that the flavour of a passage will be at times coloured by what is being read in the world of theology rather than necessarily what is being presented in the text and the grammar.

Now that there is good evidence that the doctrine of unconditional predestination was not in the church in the 1st four centuries I ask that a full review of the passages of the bible wrongly coloured be restored to the natural meaning. This ranges from added words unwarranted by the grammar and context (Romans 8:28 and 11:22) to using similar words or phrases for different Greek words (Romans 9:22-23) to assuming inspiration of lexicons – Greek word dictionaries – so that a Greek word is repeatedly misrepresented like *eklektos* and unhelpful wording (Psalm 139 and Acts 13:48), and so on. If you will honestly review these then please also consider the research done on 1 Timothy 2:12 and 1 Corinthians 11:3 as contained in my book *Leadership is male?*

For a bible society to perpetuate the practise mentioned and in the light of the source of all heresy, would that not be to bless the work of the Deceiver in his efforts to blaspheme the living God? Is it conceivable that the Lord will not judge such known activity or any effort to prevent change from that practise? Of course this applies to all involved in bible production, whether publishers or bible society executives or distributors. And the very least booksellers, churches and interested parties can do, is to voice their disapproval of any such ongoing practises. I have tried to play my part. I implore you to take up the challenge and do yours.

APPENDICES

APPENDIX 1

PROTHESIS

———

This appendix serves as added information to back up the translation of Romans 8:28 in chapter 11 entitled *Romans 8:28 in Context*

> But we know that to the ones loving God He works together all into good, for they are the ones called according to a displayed intent.
> *Romans 8:28 J. R. More*

The Septuagint (LXX) is the Greek version of the Old Testament scriptures. As found in the New Testament it is the text from which Paul and the other apostles often quoted. It is useful here in helping highlight the meaning of this Greek word found in the New Testament. Since this Greek is the same as used in the New Testament and the authors knew it, the Septuagint is a valuable tool to help ascertain meanings to words. The inspiration of the Septuagint text is not being queried, it is not an issue; the use of the words in the Greek are. And Koine Greek, as the New Testament Greek is known, has precious few examples of the language in the written records such that to have one such example as the Septuagint, also known and valued by the Lord and the apostles, makes it important and of value to take note of. See Appendix 2 for examples of New Testament quotes of the Septuagint.

The Greek word *prothesis* sometimes translated as 'purpose' is accurately also understood as 'a display' (i.e. an observed intent of the heart) since its uses in the Septuagint shows it as separate and distinct from the words *artos* (bread) and *trapedza* (table) in reference to the shewbread or, the table of the shewbread.

To help show this I now quote every reference for *prothesis* in the Septuagint and give a breakdown of the Greek to show the validity of 'a setting forth', 'a displayed intent' as a good meaning for *prothesis*.

The following passages are dealt with:

Exodus 39:18	1 Chronicles 28:16
Exodus 40:4	2 Chronicles 2:4
Exodus 40:23	2 Chronicles 4:19
1 Samuel 21:6	2 Chronicles 13:11
1 Chronicles 9:32	2 Chronicles 29:18
1 Chronicles 23:29	

Throughout the following passages *trapedza* = table and *artos* = bread (these are not in dispute), *prothesis* is however not so well recognised in the New Testament usage as 'a setting forth' or, 'a displayed intent' as I have translated it, but 'a purpose'. Also as with the note above, 'ò' = *omega* and, 'é' = *éta*.

Exodus 39:18
(N.B. Exodus 39:37-41 in our translations from the Hebrew is the area, but this passage is not included)

Kai tén <u>trapedzan</u> tés **protheseòs**,
and the <u>table</u> of **shewbread**,

Kai - tén - <u>trapedzan</u> - tés - **protheseòs**,
and - the - <u>table</u> - of the - **(of) showings**,

protheseòs = (of) showings [bread is only implied and thereby is understood as the shew-bread]

Exodus 40:4

Kai eisoiseis tén <u>trapedzan</u>, kai **prothéseis** tén **prothesin** autés
and thou shalt bring in the <u>table</u> and **shalt set forth**[c] that which is **to be set forth** on it;

kai - eisoiseis - tén - <u>trapedzan</u>, * kai - **prothéseis** - tén - **prothesin** - autés
and - you shall bring - the - <u>table</u>, * and - **(he) shall set forth** - the - **(a) setting forth** - of her;

protheseis = he shall set forth [hence the translator's note: 'Setting forth of it']
prothesin = to be set forth - [the] showing - [the] display

C: "Setting forth of it"

Exodus 40:23

Kai prosethéken ep' autés <u>artous</u> tés **protheseòs** enanti Kuriou,
And he put on it the **shewbread** before the Lord,

Kai - prosethéken - ep' - autés - <u>artous</u> - tés - **protheseòs** - enanti - Kuriou,
And - he put forth - upon - of her - <u>breads</u> - of the - **(of) showings** - before - [the] Lord,

protheseòs = (of) showings [unlike Exodus 39:18 the implication of bread is removed by stating 'bread' explicitly: thus shows *prothesis* on it's own as a showing - a display]

255

1 Samuel 21:6

Kai edòken autò Abimelech ho hiereus tous <u>artous</u> tés **protheseòs**, hoti ekei ouk én artoi, all' é artoi tou prosòpou hoi aphérémenoi ek prosòpou Kuriou,

So Abimelech the priest gave him the **shewbread**; for there were no loaves there, but only the presence loaves which had been removed from the presence of the Lord,

Kai - edòken - autò - Abimelech - ho - hiereus - tous - <u>artous</u> - tés - **protheseòs**, * hoti - ekei - ouk - én - artoi, * all' - é - artoi - tou - prosòpou - hoi - aphérémenoi - ek - prosòpou - Kuriou,

And/So - (he) gave - to/for him - Abimelech - the - priest - the - <u>bread(s)</u> - of the - **(of) showings**, * since/due to - there - no - was - breads, * but - (was) - breads - of the - (of) face [i.e. presence] - the - had been removed(s) - out of/from - (of) face [presence] - of [the] Lord,

protheseòs = of showings [Just like Exodus 40:23, but unlike Exodus 39:18 the implication of bread is removed by stating 'bread' explicitly: this shows *prothesis* on it's own as: a showing - a display]

1 Chronicles 9:32

Kai Banaias ho kaathités ek tòn adelphòn autòn epi tòn <u>artòn</u> tés **protheseòs**, tou etoimasai sabbatòn kata sabbaton.

And Banaias the Caathite, from among their brethren, *was set* over the **shewbread**, to prepare it every sabbath.

Kai - Banaias - ho - kaathités - ek - tòn - adelphòn - autòn - epi - tòn - <u>artòn</u> - tés - **protheseòs**, * tou - etoimasai - sabbatòn - kata - sabbaton.

And - Banaias - the - Caathite - out of/from - of the - (of)
brothers - of them/their - upon - the - <u>breads</u> - of the - **(of)**
showings, * of the - preparing - of sabbaths - according to
- sabbath.

protheseòs = of showings [as per 1 Samuel 21:6]

1 Chronicles 23:29

kai eis tous <u>artous</u> tés **protheseòs**, kai eis tén semidalin
tés thusias, kai eis ta lagana ta adzuma,
and for the **shew-bread**, and for the fine flour of the
meat-offering, and for the unleavened cakes,

kai - eis - tous - <u>artous</u> - tés – **protheseòs**, * kai - eis - tén
- semidalin - tés - thusias, * kai - eis - ta - lagana - ta -
adzuma,
and - into/to [for] - the - <u>breads</u> - of the - **(of) showings**,
* and - into/to [for] - the - fine flour - of the - (of) sacrifice,
* and - into/to [for] - the - cakes - the - unleavened,

protheseòs = of showings [as per 1 Samuel 21:6]

1 Chronicles 28:16

Edòken autò homoiòs ton stathmon tòn <u>trapedzòn</u> tés
protheseòs, ekastés trapedzés chrusés,
He gave him likewise the weight of the <u>tables</u> of **shewbread**[D],
of each table of gold,

Edòken - autò - homoiòs - ton - stathmon - tòn - <u>trapedzòn</u>
- tés - **protheseòs**, * ekastés - trapedzés - chrusés,

He gave - (to/for) him - like - the - weight - of the - <u>(of) tables</u> - of the - **(of) showings**, * of each - (of) table - (of) gold,

protheseòs = (of) showings/ setting forth [As per Exodus 39:18]

D: 'Gr. tables of the setting forth'

2 Chronicles 2:4

hagiasai auton autò tou thumian apenanti autou thumiama kai **prothesin** diapantos, kai tou anapherein holokautòmata diapantos topròi kai todeilés,
to consecrate it to him, to burn incense before him, and *to offer* **shewbread** continually, and to offer up whole-burnt-offerings continually morning and evening,

hagiasai - auton - autò - tou - thumian - apenanti - autou - thumiama - kai - **prothesin** - diapantos, * kai - tou - anapherein - holokautòmata - diapantos - topròi - kai - todeilés,
to consecrate - it - to/for him - of the - incense - before - of him/his - incense - and - **a showing** - continually/always by, * and - of the - to offer up - whole-burnt-offerings - continually/always by - the dawnings - and - the settings,

prothesin = a showing, a setting forth [As per Exodus 39:18]

2 Chronicles 4:19

Kai epoiése Salòmòn panta ta skeué oikou Kuriou, kai to thusiastérion to chrusoun, kai tas <u>trapedzas</u>, kai ep' autòn artoi **protheseòs**,

And Solomon made all the vessels of the house of the Lord, and the golden altar, and the <u>tables</u>, and upon them *were to be* the <u>loaves</u> of **shewbread**;

Kai - epoiése - Salòmòn - panta - ta - skeué - oikou - Kuriou - kai - to - thusiastérion - to - chrusoun, * kai - tas - <u>trapedzas</u> - kai - ep' - autòn - <u>artoi</u> - **protheseòs**,
And - he made - Solomon - all - the - vessel - of house - of [the] Lord - and - the - altar - the - golden, * and - the - <u>tables</u> - and - upon - of them - <u>breads</u> - **of showings**,

protheseòs = of showings/ of setting forths [as per 1 Samuel 21:6]

2 Chronicles 13:11

kai thumiama suntheseòs, kai **protheseis** <u>artòn</u> epi tés trapedzés tés katharas,
and compound incense, and *set* the **shewbread** on the pure table;

kai - thumiama - suntheseòs, * kai - **protheseis** - <u>artòn</u> - epi - tés - trapedzés - tés - katharas,
and - incence - compound, * and - **showed** - <u>of breads</u> - upon - of the - (of) table - of the - (of) pure,

protheseis = showed [the implication of bread is removed by stating 'breads' explicitly: this shows *prothesis* on it's own as: a showing - a display - a setting forth (i.e. an intent seen, a purpose visualised in the context of Romans 8:28)]

2 Chronicles 29:18

> to thusiastérion tés holokautòseòs kai ta skeué autou, kai
> tén <u>trapedzan</u> tés **protheseòs** kai ta skeué autés,
> the altar of whole-burnt-offering, and its vessels, and the
> <u>table</u> of **shew-bread**, and its vessels;

> to - thusiastérion - tés - holokautòseòs - kai - ta - skeué -
> autou, * kai - tén - <u>trapedzan</u> - tés - **protheseòs** - kai - ta -
> skeué - autés,
> the - altar - of the - (of) whole-burnt-offerings - and - the -
> vessel - of it, * and - the - <u>table</u> - of the - **(of) showings** -
> and - the - vessel - of her,

> protheseòs = (of) showings/ setting forths [As per Exodus
> 39:18]

Both Greek words and the initial translation quoted are taken from *The
Septuagint with Apocrypha: Greek and English* by Sir Lancelot C.L.
Brenton and published by Hendrikson Publishers, Peabody, MA. Originally
published in 1851 by Samuel Bagster & Sons Ltd, London.

Conclusion

Prothesis on it's own due to the context of the Old Testament
Septuagint passages is seen to mean 'the shewbread'. That is, the
loaves of bread which were put on a table for a symbol before the
Lord in the temple. But when the word for bread – *artos* is added
it still means just the same. This tells us that the word *prothesis* itself
is understood to mean 'a showing' or 'a display'. In it's common use
in the New Testament as 'purpose' it can thereby be also understood
as a 'display of intent' - 'a plan in view' which is in fact an equivalent
meaning for the word 'purpose' itself. A 'setting forth', a 'showing'
appears to be the core meaning with *Pro* – 'in front of' and *thesis*
– 'a view of (mental or otherwise)', such that if mental it is an idea
or theory, a plan or decided aim, a purpose – a display of intent:

God who searches the heart (Psalm 7:9; Jeremiah 17:10; Revelation 2:23), by His Spirit intercedes and then sets the individual up – predestines (as per Romans 8:26-30) – to a calling following a display of love witnessed in the heart: for **'as many as received Him, to them He gave the right to become children of God'** (John 1:12).

APPENDIX 2

EKLEKTOS

———

Matthew 20:16 – Matthew 22:14 – Matthew 24:22 –
Matthew 24:24 – Matthew 24:31
Mark 13:20 – Mark 13:22 – Mark 13:27
Luke 18:7 – Luke 23:35
Romans 8:33 – Romans 16:13
Colossians 3:12
1 Timothy 5:21 – 2 Timothy 2:10
Titus 1:1
1 Peter 1:2 – 1 Peter 2:4 – 1 Peter 2:6 – 1 Peter 2:9
2 John 1 – 2 John 13
Revelation 17:14

These are the 23 places in the New Testament where the Greek word *eklektos* is found. It has been translated as 'chosen' (7) and 'elect' (16) in English (numbers reflect the frequency in the KJV). Such that the following verses include them and are well known:

. . . For many are called, but few chosen.

Matthew 20:16 & 22:14

But you *are* a chosen generation, a royal priesthood, a holy nation, His own special people . . .   *1 Peter 2:9*

I charge *you* before God and the Lord Jesus Christ and the elect angels . . .   *1 Timothy 5:21*

For false christs and false prophets will arise and . . . deceive, if possible, even the elect.   *Matthew 24:24 & Mark 13:22*

And He will send His angels . . . and they will gather together His elect from the four winds, from one end of heaven to the other.   *Matthew 24:31 & Mark 13:27*

Who shall bring a charge against God's elect? *Romans 8:33*

I wish to bring evidence to light which shows these are inaccurate translations of *eklektos*. The writers of the New Testament used the Greek of the day as their language and as shown by their quotes of the Old Testament were well-versed in the language employed by the Greek Version of the Hebrew scripture. This is known as the Septuagint. This text reveals that *eklektos* to the common reader was understood as 'quality', 'special', 'choice' (in that sense), 'best', 'tops', etc. The flavour is one of quality and not a selection as has been understood by 'chosen' and 'elect'. This would make the above passages read like this:

For many are called, but few are fit for it.

Matthew 20:16 & 22:14 JM

But you are a quality generation, a royal priesthood, a holy nation, His own special people . . .   *1 Peter 2:9 JM*

I charge you before God and the Lord Jesus Christ and the good angels . . .   *1 Timothy 5:21 JM*

For false christs and false prophets will arise and . . . deceive, if possible, even the saints [the good guys].

Matthew 24:24 & Mark 13:22 JM

264

> And He will send His angels . . . and they will gather together
> His precious ones [the good guys] from the four winds,
> from one end of heaven to the other.
>
> *Matthew 24:31 & Mark 13:27 JM*

> Who shall bring a charge against God's precious?
>
> *Romans 8:33 JM*

Of course, since quality is the emphasis a number of possible alternatives in English give the intended flavour. As long as the 'idea' of selection as implied is removed when quality is the reality then the translation becomes more accurate and true to the original meaning intended.

Evidence that the writers of the New Testament used the Septuagint

It is of note here that the inspiration of the Septuagint is not at issue here, but the use of the Greek language in which it was translated and this being known by the writers of the New Testament. When Alexander the Great conquered the whole Mediterranean region and then the various Greek dynasties ruled, Greek became the main language of communication between peoples and for commerce. So that when the Romans then conquered the region, Greek was very much in use. The Septuagint, with the reference LXX, is the Greek translation of the Hebrew Old Testament of the Bible. Tradition has it as translated by 70 scholars hence its name. It was carried out within the period of 285-247BC in Alexandria, Egypt and became the common used Bible for Jesus, the apostles and the first Christians.

This use by the apostles and Jesus can be seen by their quotes of the Old Testament:

> Away with you, Satan! For it is written, *'You shall worship the LORD your God, and Him only you shall serve.'*
>
> *Matthew 4:10*

The Septuagint contains the words '**kai autò monò**'[1], in English '**and Him only**', and this '**only**' translated from Deuteronomy 6:13

265

is not found in the Hebrew. This is why these are not read when the Old Testament passages quoted by Jesus and the other apostles are looked up in our Bibles. Our Old Testaments are translated direct from the Hebrew.

> *'These people draw near to Me with their mouth, and honour Me with their lips, but their heart is far from Me. And in vain they worship Me, teaching as doctrines the commandments of men.'*   Matthew 15:8-9

This is a quote by Jesus primarily of Isaiah 29:13. Similar sentiments are found in Psalm 78:36 and Ezekiel 33:31. The Hebrew does not contain '**in vain they worship Me**' whilst it is there in the Septuagint '**matén de debontai me**'. This vouches therefore for Matthew and Jesus' use of the Septuagint.

A good example of Paul's use of it:

> Beloved, do not avenge yourselves, but *rather* give place to wrath; for it is written, *'Vengeance is Mine, I will repay,'* says the Lord. *'Therefore if your enemy hungers, feed him; if he thirsts, give him a drink; for in so doing you will heap coals of fire on his head.'*   Romans 12:19-20

This latter O.T. quote is direct from Proverbs 25:21-22. The Greek is exactly the same in the Septuagint as the New Testament Text. Whilst in the Hebrew Text and our Bibles Proverbs 25:21-22 reads,

> If your enemy is hungry, give him bread to eat; and if he is thirsty, give him water to drink; for so you will heap coals of fire on his head . . .   Proverbs 25:21-22

Paul makes no mention of '**bread**' or '**water**' but it is clearly there in the Hebrew. Equally he mentions '**in so doing**' which is in the Septuagint and nowhere in the Hebrew.

This common use of the Septuagint by the New Testament writers makes it a valuable resource for appreciating the meaning of words in the language of the New Testament. If a word can be clearly shown to have an emphasis different than has up till now been used, we should take notice. A revision of this translation would thereby be called upon. I believe this is the case for the adjective *eklektos*. It has been translated as 'chosen' and 'elect' giving an idea of a selection. Whilst the Greek writers used the verb *hairetizò* as in Matthew 12:18 and the verb *eklegò* as in Acts 15:22, 25 for chosen in terms of selection.

The body of proof for *eklektos* as quality

All the places where it is found in the Septuagint are mentioned. These are compared to the English translation for the Hebrew word for which the Greek translator made use of *eklektos*. The regular and common use of it for quality is readily visible.

Here follows a full list[2] of references where the word *eklektos* is to be found in the Septuagint[3]:

KEY

In bold and italics are the translations of **eklektos** involving quality.

Underlined and in italics are the translations, as quoted, involving a decision, an alternative picked.

<hr>
In borders are the translations of both types for the same Greek word.
<hr>

COMMENT

The amount of the bordered combined with the consistent **quality** emphasis show this as the normal 'feel' for the word *eklektos*. The added fact that, there is no undisputed translation with the idea of chosen, elect-ed where an individual or group of people are not involved, makes one ask what honest criteria was used to do so where individuals and particular groups are mentioned? (see chapter 5)

Reference	Greek	A Direct Translation	KJV (From the Hebrew)
Genesis 23:6	tois eklektois	our *choice* sepulchres	the *choice* of our . . .
41:2	eklektai	seven cows . . . *choice* of flesh -	*fat*fleshed
4	tas eklektas	the . . . *choice*-fleshed cows	*fat* kine
5	eklektoi	seven ears . . . *choice* and good	-*rank* and good
			[rank. Eng. in the sense of complete]
			(Heb. *fat*.)
7	tous eklektous	seven *choice* and full ears	- *rank* and full ears
18	eklektai	*choice*-fleshed	*fat*fleshed
20	tas eklektas	*choice* cows	the seven *fat* kine
Exodus 14:7	eklekta	six hundred <u>*chosen*</u> chariots	*<u>chosen</u>[4]* chariots *choice* chariots NKJV; the *best* chariots NIV
30:23	eklektés	the flower of *choice* myrrh	*pure* myrrh
Numbers 11:28	ho eklektos	Joshua . . . the <u>*chosen*</u> one	of his *young* men of his *choice* men NKJV; assistant since *youth* NIV
Deuteronomy 12:11	eklekton	every *choice* gift of yours	your *choice* vows (Heb. the *choice* of your vows.)

Book	Reference	Greek (LXX)	English (KJV)	NKJV / NIV
Judges	20:15	eklektoi	seven hundred chosen men of all the people	*chosen men / select men NKJV; chosen men NIV
	34	eklektōn	ten thousand chosen men out of all Israel	*chosen men / select men NKJV; finest men NIV
1 Samuel (LXX: 1 Kings)	24:3	eklektous	three thousand men chosen	24:2 * chosen men
	26:2	eklektoi	three thousand men chosen	*chosen men
2 Samuel (LXX: 2 Kings)	8:8	tòn eklektōn	the choice cities	N/A
	21:6	eklektous	chosen out for the Lord [the men]	the LORD did *choose (Or, chosen of the LORD.)
	22:27	eklektou	with the excellent . . .	With the pure . . . show thyself pure
	27	eklektos	. . . thou wilt be excellent	
1 Kings (LXX: 3 Kings)	3:46	eklektoi	ten choice calves	N/A See note below
	4:23	eklektoi	ten choice calves	Ten fat oxen
	23	eklektōn	and choice fatted does	and fatted fowl
2 Kings (LXX: 4 Kings)	8:12	tous eklektous	their choice men	their young men
	19:23	ta eklekta	his choice cypresses	the choice fir trees
1 Chronicles	7:40	eklektoi	choice, mighty men	choice and mighty men

It is of note that some small sections of the LXX are not found in the Hebrew scripture and therefore not in the Old Testament of our Bibles. Equally, it must be recognised that in places the translation into the Greek was 'loose' and not literal, such that when a direct counterpart in the Hebrew is non existent, the Hebrew translation into the English does not exist.

These are 2 different reasons for which N/A has been placed in the KJV column.

REFERENCE		GREEK	A DIRECT TRANSLATION	KJV (From the Hebrew)
	9:22	hoi eklektoi	All the *chosen* porters	ˆ*chosen* to be porters
	16:13	eklektoi	Jacob his *chosen ones*	his †*chosen ones*
	18:8	tòn eklektòn	out of *the chief* cities	N/A
Ezra	5:8	eklektois	with *choice* stones	with *great* stones
Nehemiah	5:18	eklekta	six *choice* sheep	six *choice* sheep
Job	37:11	eklekton	a cloud obscures [what is] *precious*	N/A
Psalm	17:26	eklektou	with the *excellent*	18:26 With the *pure* …
	26	eklektos	thou wilt be *excellent*	18:26 shew thyself *pure*
	77:31	tous eklektous	the *choice men*	78:31 the ‡*chosen* [men] the *choice* [men] NKJV; the *young men* NIV; (or, *young* men KJV)
	88:3	tois eklektois	my *chosen* ones	89:3 my †*chosen*
	19	eklekton	one *chosen* out of	89:19 * *chosen* out of; one *chosen* from NKJV; a *young man* from NIV

	104:6	eklektoi	his *chosen ones*	105:6 his †*chosen*
	43	tous eklektous	his *chosen*	105:43 his †*chosen*
	105:5	tòn eklektòn	thine *elect*	106:5 thy †*chosen*
	23	ho eklektos	his *chosen*	106:23 his †*chosen*
	140:4	tòn eklektòn	their **choice ones**	141:4 their **dainties**
Proverbs	8:19	eklektou	**choice** silver	**choice** silver
	12:24	eklektòn	*chosen men*	the **diligent** (= NKJV =NIV)
	17:3	eklektai	**choice** hearts	N/A
Canticles	5:15	eklektos	**choice** as the cedars	*excellent** as the cedars
	6:8	eklektē	the **choice** of her	6:9 the **choice** *[one]* of her
	9	eklektē	**choice** as the sun	6:10 **clear** as the sun
Isaiah	22:7	hai eklektai	*thy choice* valleys	**thy choicest** valleys
	8	tous eklektous	**the choice** houses	**the armour** of the house
	28:16	eklekton	a costly stone, a **choice**	a **tried** stone
	40:30	eklektoi	the **choice** [men]	the **young** men
	42:1	ho eklektos	Israel is my *chosen*	mine †*elect*
	43:20	to eklekton	to my *chosen*	my †*chosen*
	45:4	tou eklektou	Israel mine *elect*	Israel mine †*elect*

REFERENCE		GREEK	A DIRECT TRANSLATION	KJV (From the Hebrew)
	49:2	eklekton	a *choice* shaft	a *polished* shaft
	54:12	eklektous	*precious* stones	*pleasant* stones
	65:9	hoi eklektoi	mine *elect* and my servants	mine *elect*
	15	tois eklektois	my *chosen*	my *chosen*
	23	hoi eklektoi	My *chosen*	65:22 mine *elect*
Jeremiah	3:19	eklektén	a *choice* land	a *pleasant* land
				(Heb. land of desire)
	10:17	eklektois	*choice* [vessels]	the *fortress*
	22:7	tas eklektas	*thy choice* cedars	*thy choice* cedars
	26:15	ho eklektos	*thy choice* calf	46:15 *thy valiant* [men]
	31:15	eklektoi	his *choice* young men	48:15 his °*chosen* young (Heb. the *choice* of. . .)
	38:39	eklektòn	*choice* stones	N/A
Lamentations	1:15	eklektous	my *choice* men	my *young* men
	5:13	eklektoi	the *chosen* men	the *young* men
	14	eklektoi	the *chosen* men	the *young* men

Ezekiel	7:20	eklekta	their *choice* ornaments	the *beauty* of his ornaments
	17:22	tòn eklektòn	of the *choice* [branches] of the cedar	of the *highest* branch
	19:12	ta eklekta	her *choice* [branches]	her *fruit*
	14	eklektén	her *choice* [boughs]	her *fruit*
	25:9	eklektòn	the *choice* land	the *glory* of the country
	27:20	eklektòn	*choice* cattle	*precious* clothes (Heb. clothes of *freedom*)
	24	eklektous	*choice* stores	chests of *rich* apparel
	31:16	ta eklekta	the *choice* [plants]	the *choice* and best
Daniel	11:15	hoi eklektoi	his *chosen* ones	his °*chosen* people / his *choice* troops NKJV; their *best* troops NIV; (Heb. the people of his *choices*)
Amos	5:11	eklekta	*choice* gifts	*burdens* of wheat
Habbakkuk	1:16	eklekta	meats *choice*	meat *plenteous* (Or, *dainty*; Heb. *fat*)
Haggai	2:7	ta eklekta	the *choice* [portions] of all the nations	the *desire* of all nations
Zechariah	7:14	eklektén	the *choice* land	the *pleasant* land
	11:16	tòn eklektòn	the flesh of *the choice* [ones]	eat the flesh of *the fat*

Robert Young author of the Analitical Concordance to the Bible makes a valuable comment. In his research involving the useage of every word of Greek and Hebrew used in the Bible he more than most can testify to the reality of what *eklektos* stood for. In the introduction to the New Testament of his Literal Version[5] of the Bible, he has listed what should be read in place of certain words. He lists a minimum of 100 words with a return to the original intent alongside.

> For chosen he has put: read choice one, very often in N.T.
> For elect: read choice one, very often in S.S.

Basic analysis

There are 82 occasions where the word *eklektos* is found in the Septuagint. Of these 7 have no corresponding section of writing in the Hebrew scripture as found translated in the Old Testament. This leaves us with 75 places where the word is found.

Out of 75 places 23 have been translated from the Hebrew into the KJV as chosen (18); elect (4); choose (1).

This leaves us with 52 places where the translation (in the KJV) from the Hebrew words associated with *eklektos* are as follows:

> choice (9); young [men] (6); pure (5); fat (4); pleasant (3); rank [Eng. complete] (2); highest [branch] (1); fatted (1); great [stones] (1); diligent (1); excellent (1); clear [as the sun] (1); thy choicest [valley] (1); the armour [of the house] (1); tried [stone] (1); polished [shaft] (1); beauty (1); fruit (1); glory (1); precious [clothes] (1); rich [apparel] (1); burdens [of wheat] (1); plenteous (or, dainty) [meat] (1); the desire [of all nations] (1); valiant (1); dainties (1).

It is undisputed therefore that the Greek thinkers who put together the Septuagint saw the understanding of quality as the prominent flavour for the word *eklektos*.

As mentioned above there are however 18 places (in the KJV) where chosen is found, 3 with elect and 1 with choose from Hebrew words associated with *eklektos*. The references for these are as follows:

chosen: Exodus 14:7**; Judges 20:15**; Judges 20:34**;
1 Samuel 24:3; 1 Samuel 26:2; 1 Chronicles 9:22;
1 Chronicles 16:13; Psalm 77:31**; Psalm 88:3;
Psalm 88:19**; Psalm 104:6; Psalm 104:43; Psalm
105:5; Psalm 105:23; Isaiah 43:20; Isaiah 65:15;
Jeremiah 31:15**; Daniel 11:15**

Elect: Isaiah 42:1; Isaiah 45:4; Isaiah 65:9

choose: 2 Samuel 21:6

I have marked 7 of the references with a double star because they are translated differently in the margin of the KJV or other versions like the NKJV or NIV as follows:

Exodus 14:7	choice chariots **NKJV**	the best chariots **NIV**
Judges 20:15	select men **NKJV**	chosen men **NIV**
Judges 20:34	select men **NKJV**	finest men **NIV**
Psalm 77:31	the choice [men] **NKJV**	the young men **NIV** (Or, young men **KJV**)
Psalm 88:19	one chosen from **NKJV**	a young man **NIV**
Jeremiah 31:15 (48:15 in our bibles)	**KJV** margin: Heb. the choice of . . .	
Daniel 11:15	his choice troops **NKJV**	their best troops **NIV**

This means that 7 can reasonably be removed from the list as meaning chosen and added to the one where quality is the prime emphasis. There is doubt of a 'selection' being the emphasis.

New tally: quality (type) 59; chosen 11; elect 4; choose 1

The 'selection' words can be looked at with reference to the Hebrew words from which they are translated:

    *BACHAR   chosen (2); [excellent (1)]
    †BACHIR   chosen (8); elect (4); choose (1)
    ^BARAR   chosen (1)

Not only is BACHAR translated as 'excellent' in Song of Solomon 5:15, it is found translated in the LXX without reference to *eklektos*, as 'young men' in 2 Samuel 6:1, 1 Kings 12:21, 2 Chronicles 11:1 and Jeremiah 29:19 (49:19)

As 'mighty warriors' in 2 Chronicles 13:3 and 13:17

As 'mighty men' in 2 Chronicles 13:17

As 'youths' in Jeremiah 27:44 (50:44)

This of course brings doubt on a 'selection' emphasis.

New tally: quality (type) 61; chosen 9; elect 4; choose 1

BARAR is found in the KJV variously in regards to its root meaning of 'to clarify', 'to examine' or, 'test'.

It is found with a 'quality' emphasis in words like 'choice' (2): 1 Chronicles 7:40; Nehemiah 5:18

'polished' (1): Isaiah 49:2

'pure' (1): Zephaniah 3:9, et al.

Thus anything 'chosen' is due to its quality being discovered (after a testing).

This automatically gives us a new tally: quality (type) 62; chosen 8; elect 4; choose 1

The remainder is translated from BACHIR.

Could it be the Septuagint translators felt that BACHIR in the context they found it was understandable as 'quality' and thus used *eklektos*?

Conclusion

Suffice to say that in the 1st century a reader of the New Testament had knowledge of the Greek as found in the Septuagint. Seeing as this Old Testament Version had the fat cows that came out of the Nile in Pharaoh's dream which Joseph interpreted as *eklektos* cows. And that quality silver is *eklektos* silver. And young men (guys in their prime) are known as *eklektos*. When he read in Matthew that Jesus said 'Many are called, few *eklektos*' he fully understood that few were quality and fit for that calling. In Luke 23:35, 1 Peter 2:4 and 1 Peter 2:6 Jesus is referred to as 'chosen' and 'elect' from the word *eklektos*, since He is God in the flesh (1 Timothy 3:16), it is not a reference to His being picked from others, but His being Special.

NOTES

1 As stated before in Greek there are 2 'o's as letters. (o) omicron and (w) omega. I denote omicron with an ordinary 'o' and omega with 'ò'. Similarly there is (e) epsilon and (h) eta. I denote epsilon with an ordinary 'e' and eta with 'é'.

2 The initial list worked from was taken from A CON-CORDANCE OF THE SEPTUAGINT compiled by George Morrish and published by Zondervan. First published in 1887.

3 Both Greek words and the initial translation quoted are taken from THE SEPTUAGINT WITH APOCRYPHA: GREEK AND ENGLISH by Sir Lancelot C.L. Brenton and published by Hendrikson. Originally published in1851.

4 The following symbols have been used to identify which Hebrew word 'chosen', 'elect', 'choose' and 'excellent' were translated from: *bachar; †bachir; ‡bachur; ^barar; °mibchar.

5 YOUNG'S literal translation of the HOLY BIBLE by Robert Young Revised Edition published by Baker Book House. Third Edition January 1898.

Except for the last sentence of the conclusion the information in this appendix was first published as a booklet entitled *The Meaning of eklektos – A Request of Revision of 23 New Testament Passages*

LIST OF BIBLE PASSAGES USED